Chasing Elephants

Healing Psychologically With Buddhist Wisdom

Diane Shainberg, Ph.D.

D1310871

CHASING ELEPHANTS
Healing Psychologically With Buddhist Wisdom

By Diane Shainberg, Ph.D.

Published by:
Asti-Rahman Books
P.O. Box 674
New York, New York 10028-0044

ISBN: 0-9701585-0-5
Library of Congress Catalog Card Number: 00-91848

Manufactured in the United States of America
10 9 8 7 6 5 4 3 2 1

Cover Illustration by Itoko Maeno

Book and Cover Production by One-On-One Book Production, West Hills, California

The paper and materials used in this book met the guidelines for permanence and durability of the Committee on Production Guidelines for Book Longevity of the Council on Library Resources.

This book has been manufactured to library specifications.

Dedicated to my daughter, Nancy

Permissions

Contents

Acknowledgments

So many people have influenced my work as a psychotherapist and teacher that at times I can't separate my ideas from ideas in the world for thousands of years. I met Roshi Bernie Glassman in Los Angeles twenty-five years ago. He embodied the Buddhist view of compassion and wisdom in the moment-to-moment way of living our everyday life. He took me into situations I might never have entered and taught me how to be intimate with them. Maezumi Roshi welcomed me to UCLA at a time of crisis and showed me the natural way true nature heals when we leave things as they are.

I met Lama Surya Das seven years ago and have done Dzogchen retreats with him every year since. Surya is a friend and wonderful Buddhist teacher who teaches and lives the Dzogchen teachings that completion is found in leaving things as they are. I learned from other Dzogchen and Buddhist teachers such as Tsoknyi Rinpoche, Namkhai Norbu, Venerable Pema Chödrön, and Sogyal Rinpoche how to bring the Buddhist teachings into my life. I return to Lama Surya Das each year to imbibe his down-to-earth loving wisdom. What he has taught permeates this book and the in-the-moment psychotherapy work I discuss.

For many years I have studied and read Advaita Vedanta starting with our New York City classes with Sandra Eisenstein and then with teacher Swami Dayananda. The years of Advaita were spent with avid reading of Ramana Maharshi, Nisargadatta Maharaj, and Ramesh Balsekar. I have meditated with Maharshi's mantra for years, and I've had the privilege of meeting Ramesh Balsekar in Germany and Bombay, exploring his teachings that "consciousness is all there is." Ramesh has opened my heart and shown me the egoic sense of doership that I sometimes insist on. His brilliant, loving teachings are burning through as I now return from Bombay. Whatever the destiny of this book, he has shown, has nothing to do with "me."

So many spiritual friends have influenced me, we are all designated seekers and now all finders too. It is a great pleasure to mention those who have supported the work of the spiritual-psychological continuum. A special thank-you to Sandra Weinberg, Eve Marko, Vivian Goldstein, Ken Porter, Barbara O'Hara, Pat O'Hara, Sheila Hixon, Adam Fedder, Ann Twitty, Brenda Lukeman, Evelyn Talbot, Nancy Baker, Maggy and Dean Sluyter, John Makransky, Joel Baehr, Ann Singer, Jane Bronson, Jan Jack, Sally Gottesfeld, Neil Elson, Joan Faulkner, Jan Crawford, and Valtrout Ireland. And thanks to the wonderful friends in the Thursday group who have explored this area of healing psychologically and spiritually for many years: Freida Birnbaum, Elisa Stein, Rosanna Magarelli, Finn O'Gorman, C. C. Cotlin, David Aftergood, Carol Serigliano, Perri Fescier, Nancy Taphorn, Betsy Naylor, and Tamara Greeley. Your passionate interest in these issues has inspired me for many years.

For the past five years I studied and practiced the Diamond Heart work of A. H. Almaas. This is a path genuinely integrating spiritual and psychological work. Although the questions, inquiries, and explorations of how to end human suffering have been with us since the Buddha manifested them some people can brilliantly apply and teach them. A. H. Almaas, who began the Diamond Heart work, and Alia Johnson, my Diamond Heart teacher in New York City, are two such people. The ways A. H. Almaas has brought the Sufi and Buddhist and Vedanta paths to the work of inner transformation has had a positive and lasting effect on me.

Alia Johnson's brilliant and always creative work has interpenetrated my own. Her original, loving way of helping her students discover their freedom has colored my life beyond measure and my gratitude to her is immense. My clients have greatly benefited from the natural way she inquires into living process as it unfolds. Her loving heart opened mine.

Special thanks to my friend Elaine Norman, who has always supported my work, and to my sensitive editors, Betsy Robinson and Deborah Miller, who gave me helpful suggestions on this book with clarity and kindness. My son, Steven, and my daughter, Nancy, have taught me how to stay present and see what's happening no matter what.

I am grateful beyond words for what I can pass on from so many sources of wisdom and healing. To the Source itself I say, "Thy will be done."

Diane Shainberg

Foreword

I'm writing this book as a psychotherapist as well as a Buddhist priest. This book looks, from the perspective of a practicing psychotherapist and spiritual practitioner, at the question of how we really change. *Chasing Elephants* looks at how psychotherapy and Buddhist psychology specifically work to create inner change, and the methods presented can be used on one's own or in combination with a psychological or spiritual guide. My practice base is both Zen and Dzogchen Buddhism. I hope the encounters in the book clarify the path of healing into our inner wisdom where we can see things as they are. I hope they convey the journey within to come home to our intrinsic comfort and ease.

My own passage was from being trained as a psychoanalytic psychotherapist in the 1960s. I began my own spiritual journey with J. J. Krishnamurti. He taught me that choosing to come into the now brings us our freedom and our truth. His pure presence had a profound impact on me. The walks I had with Krishnamurti in Ojai convinced me that there is a place in us where our own being is the fullness we seek. I remember hearing thirty years ago from him, "The observer is the observed" and instantly opening into nonduality. It has taken me all these years to begin to stabilize that original opening.

I began to sit in Zen meditation as a way of giving myself "a few moments of peace." I found that stillness and staying open calmed my frantic mind. Eido Roshi from the New York Zen Center came to my home and taught a group of psychologists, psychiatrists, and social workers to sit in Zen Buddhist meditation. I sat in Zen practice with Maezumi Roshi and then became a student of Roshi Bernie Glassman, with whom I still study and with whom I ordained as a Zen Peacemaker priest.

With Roshi Glassman I learned to live in the unknown, to bear witness, and to trust staying present to realize the intimate connection with what is. With Roshi Glassman I did things I could never have imagined doing like living in a bakery, living at Auschwitz concentration camp, collecting money from everyone I ever knew for mala beads, and staying open frame by frame. Along the way I studied Advaita Vedanta with Sandra Eisenstein and Ramesh Balsekar, I became a passionate reader of Nisargadatta Maharaj, H. W. L. Poonja, Ramesh Balsekar, and Advaita Vedanta. It has been a meaningful center of my meditation practice. Some years ago I began to practice Dzogchen Buddhism with the American teacher Lama Surya Das. In New York City I teach meditation and Buddhism in a school called the Mani Center for Integral Psychotherapy. In the school, healers, therapists, counselors, and others come to learn how to bring spiritual principles, practices, and meditation into their work.

There is a continuum from the psychological into the spiritual where learning to bring awareness into the Right Now brings us to our true nature; brings us home inside where we are full and complete as we are. All of this plus the love of the people I've met along the way made a passage from my being an orthodox psychotherapist to one who sees the intimate connection between spirituality, psychotherapy, and healing.

Introduction

This is a book about discovering the inborn potentials and wisdom we have inside to change and heal ourselves. Chasing elephants is a phrase that means looking for things outside of ourselves. In this book I discuss the process of turning toward ourselves—a process where we don't chase elephants anymore. We no longer look for external solutions. We stay present, let things be, experience what is there, and in the process discover how things naturally unfold and transform.

Last year I had an experience that opened my eyes to how we heal. I was going to meet my friend for dinner at a restaurant. This was a very close friend—someone whose friendship I certainly wanted to continue, although we had been estranged for the past several months. On my way to the restaurant I felt a certain kind of pressure because I hadn't been able to help her make any connections to find a new job. It wasn't that I saw that as my particular duty, but I thought I should be able to help somehow, and she certainly thought I should. I had already introduced her to the only people I knew, and none of them had been helpful, and one had hurt her. There was a sense of unfinished business between us. There was also a bit of anger on my part that she had not put as much effort into looking for a job as I felt she should. In addition, I was feeling depressed and had been going through a lonely period. I was aware that I hoped she would cheer me up, and I began to speculate on how I wanted something from her — not only this evening but in general. Sometimes it was possible to get this from her, sometimes not. I was also aware that I didn't want to lose her. I expected her to have a period of attacking me that evening as she spoke of her unemployment, boredom, and frustrated creativity, and we'd both know the hidden agenda was that somehow I should be doing more for her. All these thoughts were going on as I approached the restaurant.

The meeting was tense, and she was in an argumentative frame of mind as she recounted how badly things were going for her. However, instead of reacting in my usual way—asking her or myself what I might be able to do—I did something different. As she described one negative situation after another, I began internally to surrender into just listening or bearing witness to her struggle. I didn't know what to do to make her life fuller. There wasn't much I could do. After listening for a while, I offered certain kinds of remarks, all of which she attacked. In the past I might have asked if she was angry at me, and she probably would have denied it. This time I didn't ask about her anger, but once again listened and recognized it. She then asked me something about how I was and I told her how life had been difficult of late. I spoke of a loss of a spiritual community along with the recent loss of a spiritual teacher, and I told her that there had not only been a lot of sadness about this but also a lot of self-blame.

There was a distinct sense of discomfort for a few moments as I realized she was not cheering me up, and she may have realized that I was not helping her out. We ordered our food and the silence seemed pregnant with disappointment. Soon after this, I realized I was beginning to relax. I was simply letting myself be where I was, and something inside me began to open. I was aware that I had not defended myself or reacted against her anger. I was aware that there was nothing that I knew to do. In knowing this, I had seen clearly and honestly how I felt. As we sat a little longer without any solutions, I felt more at ease. There was a very deep relationship between us. I sensed that an easier flow of energy had started. I had stopped chasing elephants, and I began to feel that some kind of healing was going on, things were shifting into more ease and acceptance in me. I had solved nothing. And yet there was a fullness as I let things be.

The sequence here had something to do with experiencing my emotions and being aware that I wasn't identified with them, staying present and staying open. In this process of not knowing and staying present, it seemed to me that some kind of intelligence came through me where I could see someone as they were. In this book I'm calling this the functioning of wisdom — that is, seeing things as they are. Out of this kind of seeing things as they are, a healing happens. We don't know exactly how. It is a mystery, yet we know when it is happening for we experience a fullness and openness in the moment.

When my friend and I finally surrendered to simply being present and bearing witness and leaving things as they were, we both realized at some level that we were complete as we were right then, that it was okay not to be okay. The idea of being okay, or what it would take to be okay, was simply not real. What was okay was for us to be ourselves, to be exactly where we were and to be able to be with that. In doing so, we shared the energy of being intimate and not being separated by our ideas of what is okay and what is not okay. This unity of being is the very functioning of wisdom.

In Buddhist teachings on wisdom, leavings things as they are brings forth our radiant, open presence. And when we are in touch with this presence, we act with wisdom and trust that things in our life will transform in a most intelligent way.

This is not a book about fixing, controlling, or solving problems. It is not a book about thinking. It is a book about leaving things as they are and discovering the potentials we have inside of us to support us in our own healing process.

There is this spontaneous Vajra song called "Free and Easy" by Venerable Lama Gendun Rinpoche which is in the book

Natural Great Perfection by Nyoshul Khenpo Rinpoche. This
poem inspired me to write this book:

> Happiness cannot be found
> > through great effort and willpower, but is
> > already present, in open relaxation
> > and letting go.
> Don't strain yourself;
> there is nothing to do nor undo.
> Whatever momentarily arises in the body mind
> has no real importance at all,
> has little reality whatsoever.
> Why identify with, and become attached to it,
> passing judgment upon it and ourselves?
>
> Far better to simply
> let the entire game happen on its own,
> springing up and falling back like waves —
> without changing or manipulating anything —
> and notice how everything vanishes and
> reappears, magically, again and again
> time without end.
>
> Only our searching for happiness
> prevents us from seeing it.
> It's like a vivid rainbow which you pursue
> > without ever catching,
> > or a dog chasing its own tail.
>
> Although peace and happiness do not exist
> > as an actual thing or place,
> > it is always available
> > and accompanies you every instant.
>
> Don't believe in the reality
> > of good and bad experiences;
> > they are like today's ephemeral weather,
> > like rainbows in the sky.

Wanting to grasp the ungraspable,
  you exhaust yourself in vain.
As soon as you open and relax this tight fist
  of grasping,
Infinite space is there — open, inviting and
  comfortable.
Make use of this spaciousness, this freedom
  and natural ease.
Don't search any further.
Don't go into the tangled jungle
looking for the great awakened elephant
who is already resting at home
In front of your own hearth.

Nothing to do or undo.
Nothing to force,
nothing to want
and nothing missing —

Emaho! Marvelous!
Everything happens by itself.

Happiness, this poem says, is already present. It is our natural state when we relax the structures of the mind that develop from grasping on to a "me" and a "you" concept. When we see that so many of us are looking for happiness externally, it becomes important to encourage ourselves to look within, to learn to recognize what is within. The possibilities of turning inward, and the suffering that occurs when we focus externally is what I discuss in Chapters 1, 2, and 3. In these first three chapters I discuss what we find inside to heal when we stay present. Passing judgment on ourselves and straining to become something other than what we are is a strain and doesn't let us rest at ease inside. Our awareness of our inner process brings us to our intrinsic inborn happiness. Learning to "let the entire game happen on its own" is learning to have faith and trust in what is inside of us.

What is there to trust inside ourselves? I discuss this question in Chapters 4, 5, and 6. To trust our own process, our natural flow, is to discover what we have inside as our natural healing powers. Then healing is based on potential, resiliency, and the natural healing wisdom of our awakened heart-mind. Psychotherapy has often emphasized deficiency. Buddhist wisdom emphasizes our true human nature where we have everything we need to heal. We can learn to relax and open and stop chasing elephants when we pause to recognize what we already have.

Chapter 7 looks at what Buddhist wisdom can teach regarding change and healing. Chapter 8 looks at how we heal into our pure presence where we can rest and be at ease. Leaving things as they are doesn't mean we don't have to use skillful means to encourage this process of healing to take root inside. This process of not searching outside ourselves is not to say we don't go on as we have — being a seeker, if that is who we are. It does mean, however, that we want to discover what is "open, inviting and comfortable" inside when we stay present in our experience. Staying present and open is to truly grasp how everything transforms on its own when we can let it be.

Much of my life I have been an elephant chaser, going into the jungle in many countries before I was willing to come home to my own breath and awareness and dance of consciousness in front of my own hearth. Many people have inspired me to turn within, to stay present, and to bear witness. Here I don't know what's going to happen and

> "*Emaho!* Marvelous!
> Everything happens by itself."

❧ ❧ ❧

Endnotes

Nyoshul Khenpo Rinpoche and Lama Surya Das, *Natural Great Perfection* (Ithaca, NY: Snow Lion Publications, 1995), pp. 11-12.

Leaving Things as They Are

Pure awareness without judgment or opinion is called true nature in Buddhism. True nature is the open space of pure potentiality. From this open space of awareness within us springs forth the endless display of life. In this open space of our awareness we can hold whatever life brings us without being reactive. In this space of nonjudgmental, clear, vividly awake awareness we discover that we have the wisdom and compassion, the knowing and clarity that innately is our true human nature. Only the discovery of the space of our true nature within can bring us a lasting contentment, peace, clarity, and love. In this space of open awareness our inherent potentials wait in seed form to emerge and bring us everything we need in order to heal into our unique and universal Being.

The discovery of the many healing potentials that our true nature brings to us has not been recognized or validated in psychology. People long to discover their spiritual roots, for they sense that who they are is not totally in the ego or the personality that they've been trained to assume. When we find our spiritual source as awake awareness inside, we can be open in the middle of all that life brings us. Our pure open awareness within each moment is the fullness we are seeking. When we rest in awareness, then seeing, hearing, thinking, smelling, feeling, touching, and tasting brings us to a flow of living where we can be vividly alive without grasping. The spirit within as our vital essence, our fresh unborn awareness, will support us by sending us specific potentials that we were born with, to use as we need them.

In our true nature are inborn in all of us the potentials of clarity, self-value, intelligence, power, wisdom, love, and wakefulness. Within us innately at birth are also the potentials of confidence, sexuality, pleasure, basic goodness, staying present, and compassion. When we need to heal, these inborn potentials naturally come forth to support us. We are also born with the intrinsic potentials of creativity, strength, joy, openness, spontaneity, curiosity, selflessness, humor, connectedness, truth, immediacy, gratitude, intuition, knowingness, ease, brilliance, attention, peace, contact, and endurance. To bring this group of inborn potentials to release for our healing when needed, we always work with the basic human potential of staying present and immediacy in any moment. These basic human potentials are what allow us to be fully human.

We make space for these potentials to unfold in our life as we relax our identifications with images and beliefs, judgments and concepts, and begin to let go of holding on. Leaving what comes up in us as it is, and resting our weary mind will bring us the very next thing to be revealed in our journey toward the freedom to be as we are.

When you are at the beach, you see the vast blue sky, the ever-moving waves rising and falling. You give yourself a few moments to smell the air, feel the sun's warmth. You feel the sand beneath your body. You allow your weary mind to rest and let yourself be. You stop expecting and are simply present, letting yourself experience what you are sensing and thinking and feeling right now. You may begin to feel that you are finally at rest, content, at peace. You do not have to add anything to what is happening or take anything away from it. It is complete as is. You are not worried or thinking about what you have to do this afternoon for you are simply going to let yourself be. You are aware of the great perfection all around

you: the air, earth, sky, water and sun, your vital breath, the sounds, smells, sights, tastes.

The sound of the waves is ever changing. As you look out over the water there is no sense of "you." There is relaxed open looking. Thoughts pass through as waves sparkle in the sun and you let them come and go...for they arise and go on their own. They liberate themselves when you leave them be. Each thought wants to come and then go like the waves, with its own rhythm. Everything appears and disappears spontaneously with no effort. You don't feel like grasping or expecting or fearing or wanting or hiding. You begin to trust that the next moment will unfold however it does. You are resting in the midst of it...you are returning to your awareness of the sky, of the vast openness of it. Your awareness lightly holds the sights, sounds, smells, touch, within it, and you relax into letting the world reveal itself to you without forming judgments or opinions.

You are not going to construct any stories about how life should be, for you are on the beach and you are open to receiving the nurturance that naturally comes from nature, letting it all happen; it comes as it comes and goes as it goes. Each moment brings fresh smells or sounds or shifts of lights or thoughts or a breeze or the warmth of the sun. When we are relaxed, the natural state of our true nature, our spirit, unfolds a never-ending treasure house of sensations, perceptions, feelings arising, thoughts floating through like bubbles...all coming and going in a rich spontaneous flow.

You can let your images, identities, stories, arguments, future worries, self attacks, obsessions, and wanting alone a few minutes. For now...on the beach...this is it! For now the heavens and earth are your friends, your awareness is your home, and you feel content. You are resting now, going back to what you are aware of every once in a while. You know that this is how it truly is in this place without strategies or designs…this natural world is great and full when you let yourself be. You are a part of it; you are where the action moves from; it is all there unfolding within you when you are awake to it. You have no "self" to hide or protect or find here. You are spontaneously, joyously, openly present in this vast place of light, unbounded, centerless, calm, open as the sky and sea. You let your thoughts come and go and they appear and dissolve in their own spontaneous natural way. Where do they go to? When you don't get involved with them, they appear, are recognized, and disappear into whatever they come from. You are at peace.

You return to your body and you are aware again of the warm sand on the back of your heels. You are seeing the light of midafternoon in naked clarity. You are allowing the energy of life to move through you. Your breath breathes itself without effort. Your eyes move easily for there is nothing you have to do or accomplish. You see without having to grasp any object in view. Your eyes stop at a boy on the right with green trunks, and you look at him, seeing them. He digs with such intensity, his small frame all absorbed. He is probably seven or eight. He is immersed in the digging. His shiny hair, blond and full, falls in his face, his lips are softly open taking in air. The tiny hairs on his leg move so slightly in the afternoon breeze. You notice this. He is throwing the sand out of the pail with firework eagerness. The sand jettisons in the air making arcs and being reabsorbed just as your thoughts, as your breath, as his arms, as the waves, as the moving light and shadows on the sand. This is all a part of you. You see no inside or outside. It is just happening. You are intimately in it.

"Oh, my God," you say, and know how perfect it is right now. For no reason tears form in your eyes, and a few fall down to remind you of this precious life you live. There is so much beauty pouring in. You are so full, you tremble. And you want to tell the boy how good he is, and let him know that

you are also. You want to tell him that you love all of this, including him.

Your heart opens and you look directly at the sky. You see it wherever you look, pure and open, giving you everything it has, without upset...nothing bothers it. You are now without armor or enemies or talents or tactics or plans. You have lost track of who you are. You are pure awareness, bringing you whatever you need to simply be.

Your eyes move to the tiny grass blades in front of you, not more than six of them. They are bright green and offering themselves to you this afternoon, waving swiftly and dancing right and left saying hello to you. They come to you on this day as a delicate part of the dance. You feel intimate with these grasses, you know them very well. How they embrace the moment and dance for you. You have never once seen their beauty before, seen how they dance together in sweeping lively sways. You know their tenderness well. It is within you, too.

You feel a waft of something beginning in you. It is hard to tell. You want to touch further. You want to hear what is there in you. You are opening into a depth that has no words...life unlived, many unspoken words, so much love in you, heart breaking opening into seeing. Tears pour through without expecting. A spontaneous prayer comes forth, "Magnificent... thank you, thank you." And that is the end of the prayer for the grasses and the boy and yourself, for everyone. "How much, how much, how much," thoughts spontaneously move through and dissolve. You remember somewhere reading the words of the Buddha on awakening, "How wonderful, how wonderful."

Now being aware again of the sound of the waves, you spontaneously think, "I can't miss," and with a flash you know you must arrange to be free for a time each day for stillness. There is clarity and wisdom and kindness in this knowing. The insight comes through spontaneously and is familiar, true.

The air stirs a breeze. You see so clearly and radiantly that it must be wisdom itself. You lie here openly, nakedly aware, letting all confusion and distraction liberate themselves away naturally.

In these moments on the beach you are living the spiritual teaching of the Buddha, for you have seen in pure awareness things as they are and you have tasted the great perfection we see when we are open and stay present and aware. Out of leaving things as they are, you naturally open into intimacy and compassion with the boy, the grass, yourself. You open into clarity, love, peace, awakeness, connection, self-value, and immediacy. You are one with every manifestation on the beach, for you have stopped separating yourself into an "I" and "them." Out of this silence you have stayed in your flow until a fullness comes through out of your home base of pure awareness. Here you can rest and be content. In a state of awareness you don't know how life should go. You are open to finding out from a space within that reveals itself to you in your flow.

Your spirit, your being, your awareness has come forth to welcome you to this life, to the perfection of the moment. Come present, be aware…accept the invitation.

Discover your innate vivid wakefulness and let it continue to unfold. Now you will discover the treasures from within.

After many years as a psychotherapist, I see that psychotherapy is basically a way to be with people so that they can inquire into their life and can stay present with what's arising and thus be more aware and awake in their life. Being aware, they enter inside themselves and pay attention and don't abandon themselves and give more value to what's happening externally. People in therapy begin to realize that they have lost the home inside themselves where they can find a resting place. They have lost the potential to stay present to make contact with where they are within. They have stopped the flow inside by grasping onto their stories. Structures of mind…self-concepts, self-images, identities have blocked the flow.

Clients I see have lost contact with their natural flow bringing them the aliveness they seek. They suffer a sense of isolation. They lack the freedom and trust to act within the wisdom of their own truth of the moment. Many clients I see do not feel much interest in being with themselves, except to accomplish things that will bring objects or people to them from the outside. They sense that something is missing. This is what I hear all the time: "Something is missing." How can something be missing from a moment when you are fully present in it?

As people face what they are aware of in the moment as their own experience inside their body, fear often comes up. When people grasp that the truth of where they are in the present moment is the only place to start from, they see the value in opening to their experience of fear. When they are encouraged to remain present in their fear, it shifts, and they are surprised that they end up in a completely new place for having faced fear.

Therapy, like most of life's truths, is paradoxical. We run away from what we most yearn for — to be ourselves, to find our own truth of the moment, to open to love. Clients run from being fully present in their experiences, for they don't want to find out how unhappy they are and how much love is inside them that wants to be expressed. Most clients don't want to see that they have to be responsible for the creation of their life moment to moment and that it is their clinging to their ideas and stories that make them unhappy.

People's stories say that without their mother's or mother substitute's care they will not make it, that they have nothing in this life to support them, to trust. People do not want to be still and find out what there is to trust in the universe inside themselves and outside. Buddhist wisdom teaches that there will be a discovery of innate potentials within and that pain will go away on its own when we experience it. The inner world, the world of the senses and feelings, the natural world arising within — is a vague blur to most people, who have trouble being present to their experience for moments without grabbing at a story or memory, or another person or an object, or an E-mail or drink to prop them up. It is hard for people to grasp the realization that how things are right now is all there is. However it is, it will always change and unfold and shift. We learned deeply as children to focus on becoming more and better and not to connect with what is here right now.

Throughout therapy, we bring clients to their awareness with a hundred variations on the question "What are you experiencing right now"? Where else is there to go other than right here with things as they are?

Our innate potentials are often in hiding since our childhood. Our suffering relates to not being awake and aware right in the middle of the moments we are living. The illusion is that our life comes from places and people outside of us — from others, from objects.

As clients can stay present, they start to understand how they were taught to live life on the basis of images of how other people see them. These images or costumes or pretenses take a lot of time or effort to construct, and most of our energy to maintain: "I am a cheerful, successful, and important person" is a commonly held image. Our images may have nothing to do with how we actually are. They are a drain on us.

Therapy begins to look at where we are right now in our feelings and thinking and bodily sensations. Therapy inquires into the obstacles we have as mental structures that obstruct us from seeing, experiencing, and expressing where we are in the present. Paradoxically, the images we cling to were originally used as a protection in our family, but they end up imprisoning us and taking all our energy to maintain. Only by being aware and honest in the moment can we feel we are where the action is.

Michael wants to be a woman. He is involved in voice lessons, hormones, and electrolysis. He is six feet three and learning to walk in high heels. He comes to my office and rehearses speaking and walking as a woman, changing his clothes in the bathroom. He teaches math at a university. A brilliant only child, he grew up in a studio apartment with his mother after his father left the family when he was three. His mother was a high school math teacher and an ardent stamp collector who slept in bed with him snuggling and crying over her life until he moved out at eighteen. He says he wants to be someone else. He spends three or four hours a day masturbating. He is terrified to be with himself and goes out constantly to transvestite parties, clubs. He spends hours picking out his female clothes, grading papers, doing math puzzles, and masturbating. He says he cannot be alone for a moment without touching his penis. He is afraid of returning to the "vortex," the dark studio apartment in Park Slope he grew up in, dressing up in mommy's clothes until she came home from school. Michael's mental activities are his companions, his fantasies, his friends, and his "buddy penis" he calls his "filler upper." He has only a vague idea what it is to be present with his inner bodily experience as it is arising, and to let it exist. When Michael first made contact with his feelings he did not know they were in him. They were accompanied by elaborate

visual images of darkness, or being held down, or being beaten. Michael was surprised one day when it was raining that rain had a "sound" with it. He had seldom, if ever, experienced silence without mental math or obsessing. The stillness, he said, felt like death, for awareness of stillness carries for him the emotional state of being stuck all alone and deficiently empty without a flow of inner experience in his apartment waiting for his mother. Michael has frozen the flow of life and doesn't live an inner life of sensation or feeling. He lives in compulsive thinking, repetitive fantasies where he is sought after, cared for, admired, and wanted for his gorgeous physical appearance in which he is an irresistible woman.

It is at moments terrible for me to see Michael working so hard to become someone else, and not appreciating the way he is. His moment-to-moment anger at what he is negates his very existence. He is brilliant and does not let his intuitive intelligence move through him to where he values it, or contacts it. He stops and commands all the flow through his head, always "thinking" how he will become content and free only when he is someone else.

Aren't we all doing this, trying to become someone else through our ideas of who we have to become? How often can we really be who we are spontaneously and know how wonderful that is. Don't we have to make contact with our experience, to accept our life? Don't we have to connect with what is here to know we are enough?

Bob and Cindy arrive in a chauffeur-driven car. Cindy has gray hair and enormous brown eyes. She is elegantly dressed with the softest leather shoes and purse. She is a tad taller than Bob and her voice is like gravel. She seeks to create a rapport

with me by leaning forward as she shakes my hand, almost bowing. Her eyes sink deep into mine as she tells me the good things she has heard about me. Bob hardly notices me. He tips his head a notch, but does not look at me. Bob asks me when we'll be finished so he can tell his driver. He assures me he will stay as long as he has to as this therapy is very important.

Bob and Cindy have three children, a maid, a baby-sitter, a cook, and three houses. Bob is a lawyer who in the first session tells me he made several million dollars last year. His father was a famous lawyer, and he speaks of carrying a large firm on his shoulders with a partner who isn't there and many associates who "do nothing." He tries to please me, is fast, brilliant, hostile, and arrogant with me. He tells me how he hasn't touched his wife for three years, which is when she remembered she had been "possibly incested."

Bob speaks nonstop about how he would do anything for Cindy, as she is the only woman he has been with for fifteen years and he wants no other woman. He paints himself as a victim and then viciously attacks Cindy for freezing him out. He tells me of his mood disorder and his ups and downs. His brother is a psychopharmacologist who tried him on several anti-depressants, all of which made him sleepless, manic, or which didn't work. Bob says he "isn't asking for kisses or hugs, just decency" from Cindy. He describes Cindy as frantic of late with her healers, therapist, therapy training program, and "spiritual people." He says Cindy has decided to speak to "her people" and not to him. Her various therapists have told him that she needs a "period of healing" from her past traumas, and it won't do any good to try to push her as she "has to heal at her own rate." For him this translates to no affection, "a freeze-out on her terms." Bob does not look at Cindy while he talks. She is quiet and has her head down while he speaks.

At some point after thirty minutes of Bob speaking of his pain in getting no affection, Cindy looks at me, raises her eyebrows, and says nastily, "Is it my turn"? Cindy speaks of Bob's arrogance and how he treats her like a slave. His absorption in his work is intense, and he expects her to give up her life and think about him. She feels angry at him for his fifteen years of taking her for granted and tirading like a lost child when his demands are not met at home. She speaks of his constant social demands on her, his incessant obsession with his work. Cindy refuses to have "sex on demand" when they have no closeness. Three years ago she began her own therapy, and realized she isn't interested in Bob as a lover.

She has been trying to tell him for months that she doesn't think they "have" a marriage, but he won't listen to her. He tells her to "work on it." She is busy with her kids, her own therapy training, running three houses, his parents who are sick, and she doesn't care about much else beyond the well-being of her kids. She is "deathly afraid" Bob will turn on her and take away his money and her kids if they separate. Each time she mentions it, he says he will "terrorize" her, and she won't get a cent from him. He says he will definitely take the kids because she must have a lover because no one can live without sex, and he is "ready to jump out of his office window most days." Bob tells me he takes care of everyone, and he names a long list of people, including the people in his office. He tells me his wife is a liar because she really doesn't "work" on anything. She just turns her back on him in bed and occasionally cries. He, on the other hand, has been patient and kind and will continue to "have hope."

Cindy tells me Bob doesn't hear her, and refuses to listen to her wish to separate. Cindy says she is sorry about how she is, but she is unable to warm up to Bob as "he isn't there. I don't know where he is," she says.

Bob and Cindy have known each other for fifteen years. They no longer know how to be together as people, to just be with one another without planned activities. They relate image to image. They spend no time alone together. Cindy has found a way of freedom in which she does what she wants; the clinker is that Bob pays.

They are constantly going, doing, playing off being a charming high-living, moneyed couple in New York City. The shell works well. The fact that for years they have been strangers to one another has just begun to sink in for her. Bob does not see how Cindy is a little girl who expects to be taken care of, as she is frozen in terror by intimacy except with her children. Cindy does not see or feel Bob's clutching and clawing at her as his only way to feel he might get love. Cindy does not understand that Bob is alienated from his own presence and lives strictly out of his personality.

The dynamics, patterns, acting out of object relations, images, identities, and props of this couple are right there front and center. He moves against, then clings, then feels victimized out of an internal sense of abandonment and rejection. She charms only skin deep with her looks and surface warmth, then withdraws from intimacy for fear she will be eaten up alive by his demands, his underlying cold arrogance, her fear of making contact, his inner emptiness, and his inability to just be, to experience his own being.

Cindy is aware that she feels like a little girl asking to be taken care of out of her sense of limited self-value and her fear of staying present in relating. Bob is not aware of his emotional absence. He is not aware of not being there as an authentic person. He is always playing the famous lawyer, the great father, the unloved husband, the caretaker to everyone, or the good man sacrificing for his family. These are his costumes, images, identifications, lies. His absence of being real makes Cindy agitated and lonely, but she doesn't know what it is, what to call it. She tells me she has never "exactly" been in love with Bob although she loves him. He just gets busier and busier and she doesn't want to go along for the ride, except for her kids. She is currently deciding whether to go along for them she tells me.

After a few months, I begin some sensory awareness practices with Bob and Cindy. I asked them to make eye contact in silence and stay present looking at each other a few minutes. Then I asked them to begin to touch each other's shoulders and rest their hands there and let themselves experience this. I ask, "How far will you let Bob affect you"? "How far will you let Cindy affect you"? They do this exercise in silence.

One day they take turns lying on my healing table. I ask Bob to lay his hands on Cindy's head, then her heart, then her pelvis, then legs and feet. Then Cindy brings her hands to Bob in the same places when he lies down. This is done in silence. There is a request that each remain open and aware with their experience and be in stillness for twenty minutes during the practice to be aware of exactly what they experience when they make contact.

The sensory awareness sessions bring out a tenderness in Bob. He tells me this is the first time he has been able to touch his wife in years without fear. He lets in Cindy's touch when he is lying down and has memories of her as a young woman and recalls their early years of coming together as a couple. He remembers he always felt she didn't love him, and he still feels she doesn't.

Cindy, on the other hand, is not able to let Bob's touch "in" when she is on the table. She feels his intense need for her and says this puts her off. She feels he is not much there, and she wants someone more present. It is at this point in talking that Cindy cries deeply. She doesn't feel Bob can join her in her life journey. Cindy feels how she runs from being touched, but she now feels Bob as someone deadened to feelings. She says he doesn't "come forth." Bob screams and cries, "Why"?

"Why"? and "I want to work on myself." He gives many examples of his sacrifices for her. When she remains unmoved, he storms out of the office, then comes back to tell me he doesn't know what Cindy is talking about. Cindy is talking about his not being real. He cannot be himself. He has to play roles and spin self images. He cannot stay present and just be as it arises in the moment.

Being present in the moment in the next session, Bob sees that Cindy doesn't love him. Maybe she can't love, he says, although she loves her kids. Cindy says she doesn't want to open to him anymore. She is tired of "always trying." She has found a good place inside of herself, and it doesn't include Bob. Maybe she won't find another man to love. She says she wants Bob in her life for her kids, but not romantically. "I don't love you," she says calmly. "I'm pretending it's okay, but it isn't." Bob jumps up and leaves the room, slams the door and comes back a few minutes later, saying, "I can't do this anymore. We'll work out a separation. Go look for an apartment. I can't do this to myself anymore." Bob sits in his chair quietly, looking at the floor. He looks reflective.

Cindy looks out the window. These are moments of poignant silence. There is a mutual surrender into the moment in which they feel real. Here is a moment of truth. In this moment of letting things be as they are, both partners heal spontaneously into what is happening. From this moment Cindy is clearer, stronger, more present. Bob is a bit more present, and more open and authentic. These new potentials of strength and immediacy come out of their staying present in the moment. In these moments of truth, of leaving things as they are, there's nothing to do or undo, and everything happens by itself naturally as it is meant to happen; the only way it could happen. Every event that happens reflects the functioning of totality.

After many months of therapy, an authenticity of being themselves happens between these two people.

What to call this, that emerges out of the silence between them, this presence in which their being will not be manipulated by anyone, their inner wisdom leaves things as they are? In moments of openness, such as these between Bob and Cindy, there is never right and wrong, good or bad, nor is there a reaching for anything to be concluded or interpreted.

Recognizing and leaving things as they are and surrendering into moments of letting them be, Bob and Cindy finally opened to where they were in their immediate direct experience — the truth of the moment.

Cindy is tired of trying, Bob cannot do this to himself anymore. Now they are in the openness of what Zen Buddhism calls "beginners' mind."[1] They have gone down inside and have discovered the strength and compassion to be real in the moment. They are in two different places. They have given themselves a space within to be themselves. How will this end? There is no way to know, but if they remain honest in their experiences they will find compassion for themselves, and a greater clarity, strength, and power in living together or apart. They have both accepted the invitation to move into the flow of their inner experiencing and process of unfolding.

Spirit, as I use it, refers to "what a thing is, its nature or its *vital essence*." It is called in the *Shorter Oxford English Dictionary* "the transformative agent within a person."[2] It is that aspect of us that allows transformation to occur. It is that which brings the dance of consciousness to us and makes us aware of our steady stream of changing thoughts and feelings. Spirit is the space of vital awareness in us in which we hold the world brought to us by our five senses, our feelings, and thoughts. It is that which holds it all. Spirit is contacted when we come into the present, show up and open our awareness to what is happening right now. We are being spiritual when we are fully present and awake. Spirit is called our true nature in Buddhism. It is not in essence separated into a subject and object, and it is not conditioned by the past. Our spirit will naturally unfold and bring us new specific potentials when our clinging to ego structures doesn't get in the way.

Spiritual is the same as the felt sense "That is it!" Spirit knows that this moment is all there is, and spontaneously arises from a source within that we don't control. There is a space in consciousness to see clearly what is happening and to act with the wisdom appropriate to the moment. When we are in the open space of purely being present— just a sense of "I am," or I exist—we are empty of ideas of how life is supposed to be going for us. It is extremely rare that we have a conversation with anyone and listen carefully to what *they* are saying without forming an opinion, just listening openly and respecting their point of view and hearing *them* without wanting to get something in, prove something, manipulate, seduce, convince, withdraw, or compete. It is rare that we are completely *there* in *just being* without knowing how things will go. Not knowing and listening are basic conditions of spontaneous healing.

Awareness is there to give us a fresh start a million times a day. Awareness is open and holds what life brings to us without being upset or reactive. Awareness is that which holds it all. You can't live the next moment. Frame by frame, we only have this moment.

By returning to our awareness, to our breath, our seeing and hearing, being aware of what thoughts or feelings or sensations are there, we come back into our life each moment. There's nothing we have to add or take away from the moment. We can handle what life throws us, for there is always support in the form of our potentials emerging inside. Since everything is always changing in our awareness, nothing is ever stuck and everything in our life is workable. We always have a fresh start in the now to see how we want to move, what we want to decide, how we can correct our situation, alter our perception, or take no action for the moment, and so on.

Psychotherapy has been so fragmented, cut off from the body, from allowing an exploration of the senses, so cut off from an appreciation of the functioning of awareness where we all share the human condition of impermanence and this precious human birth.

Whenever you get into a hard time within by grasping on to a story or belief or object-relations pattern, return to your awareness, be still a few moments…and check in with your energy and senses, and see and hear what is happening in your awareness right now. Come into the present moment and check it out. See what is happening. Staying in your energy allows you to release the grasp the story has on you. When you are obsessing or dwelling on negative thoughts, recognize that *you are creating your unhappiness* now, and choose to lay the story aside. We are whole and complete in each moment when we remain present. We know how to be, how to act, when we remain open, aware, and value our experience of the moment. "Pure awareness of nowness," Sogyal Rinpoche says in *The Tibetan Book of Living and Dying*, "is the real Buddha."[3]

It is not only what we didn't get as children that limits our life, it's that we haven't discovered what we have. We sometimes need a guide to help us discover what we have, someone who knows the innate potentials we have inside, and who can validate them as they come forth and can encourage us to recognize their great support for us. We discover that they come forth naturally as we leave things as they are. Wisdom and compassion always arise when we recognize and let our pain be and open into it.

I use the phrase *object relations* in this book to mean the relationship we have in our mind with another person. This other person in our mind has the power to influence our emotional state and also our behavior. Our object relations are those relations we carry in our mind with other people. These are psychic representations of particular people. We carry these people around in our head.

Jay Greenberg and Stephen Mitchell say of these inner people in our head:

> In different theoretical systems they are called variously "internal objects," "Illusory others," "introjects," "personifications" and the constituents of a "representational world" ... [They are] a source of internal security and resource invoked in times of stress and isolation.[4]

෪   ෪   ෪

Healing happens when we appreciate the Buddha within each person, using skillful means to help a person hear his- or herself, bearing witness to what is happening, listening without judgment and opinion, making psychological sense out of the obstacles presented, working with ongoing bodily or emotionally felt experiential process, and knowing how to translate the process of healing into words. The same form of work will, of course, not do for everyone. Some benefit from bodywork and imagery, some from breathing, some mystical poems, some intellect, some casual talk, some intellectual talk, some mixture…but all people need the wisdom from a therapist in which they can be seen for the amazing and potentially splendid beings they are. Each person is a perfect representation in the universe of how they are, with a particular vibration in the earth's totality. When given a space to be themselves, to be aware of their process, to see how nothing lasts, and that everything can begin anew, and to see how everything self-liberates when we don't hang on to it, each person will begin to spontaneously heal.

To be aware of where we are now, to have that noticed, recognized, welcomed, heard, and given space is the ground for healing. Buddhist wisdom teachings say that *suffering ends as we begin to give space to being where we are, noticing and respecting it, leaving it as it is instead of trying to fix it, analyze it, or make it better. This happens because the nature of the mind liberates everything that arises when we don't hold onto it.* This is a *spiritual* view of life, giving a space of great appreciation to how it is. Buddhist teaching emphasizes that whatever is there will transform naturally into a new form of energy and process when we let it be and are aware of it and commit to staying there open in it without acting out old past programs. Buddhism teaches us that the true nature of our mind is to be awake.[5] We need a process in healing that can return us to our natural spontaneous healing flow of experience and mindfully bring us to noticing how everything is arising, existing, and passing away, with a wisdom that is mysterious and a soundness that is harmonious.

Our natural human flow of consciousness gets blocked by self images, identities, judgments, early life object relations, beliefs and super-ego attacks coming from early life relation-ships still acted out and held on to as habitual mental activity.

Therapy in a spiritual context works to loosen these structures by becoming aware of them and emphasizes that they imprison the truth of who we are. Therapy in a spiritual context understands what our healing potentials are as they naturally unfold in the openness and mutual respect of the therapist/client's heart-mind connection.

There is something in us that loves truth and connection. There's something in us that wants to connect with the world in a real way, a way that reflects who we are, a way that is coming from that which is most open and alive in us. There is a place in us that knows of our true being and the happiness that it is just to exist on this earth, in a state prior to all conditioning.

The process of trusting our spiritual wisdom within, as our awareness opens to hold and accept more of our totality, and discovering the potentials we already have is the work this book discusses. We are asked in the healing process to accept the invitation to open our heart-mind and stay present. Moving into awareness in the now shows us that we always have new possibilities arising in the present moment. We are living in an incredible balance of psychological and spiritual forces. A therapist who has worked both psychologically and spiritually knows how to work in the human totality of obstructive mind structures, vivid awakeness, experiential process, spiritual wisdom potentials, and a loving heart. We need people to inspire us to turn toward ourselves, to encourage us to be aware of what's happening, to leave things as they are, and to naturally let them unfold. In this way we discover the great wisdom that lies within. In this way we can begin to discover where the elephants we've been chasing actually are.

         ॐ   ॐ   ॐ

Endnotes

1. Shunryo Suzuki, *Zen Mind, Beginner's Mind* (New York: Weatherhill, 1997), p. 22.

2. *Shorter Oxford English Dictionary, Third Ed.* (London: Oxford University Press, Amen House, 1956), pp. 1973.

3. Sogyal Rinpoche, *The Tibetan Book of Living and Dying* (New York: Harper Collins, 1994), pp. 44.

4. Jay R. Greenberg and Stephen A. Mitchell, *Object Relations in Psychoanalytic Theory* (Cambridge, MA, and London, England: Harvard University Press, 1983), p. 11.

5. Tulku Urgyen Rinpoche, *Rainbow Painting* (Boudhanath, Hong Kong and Arhus: Yale Publications, 1995).

2

Our Inner Treasures

"The only way I can justify my life is to be seen by one person. I want a relationship so good that it makes what's happened up to now not matter. I'm tired of working on my issues with men cause there aren't any. I'm mad that I haven't got what I want. That's not a problem."

Jenny is at the heart of the matter. She is aware of being tired, wanting, and pissed. She is frustrated and understands that none of this is a problem. Her wisdom is seeing things as they are. However she is still caught in a story that tells her she must have a relationship and that her life has to be justified. Without a relationship, she will not leave herself alone. She batters and criticizes herself, worries, obsesses about how to make it happen. She believes this is what will make her complete.

Each of us has a story we are identified with. We take the story to be reality. As a therapist, I speak to Jenny of her wanting, how she senses it in her body. I mention her clarity, her knowing where she is right now, her creativity and her emerging compassion for herself. We also discuss how she thinks she has to justify her life. We talk of her longing to be seen and loved and the kind of sensations coming up inside her body, the kinds of energy moving in her body. We discuss the history of her idea that she has to be in a relationship with a man to be full and complete. We speak of her exhaustion, and her history of not valuing her longing, her frustration in not getting what she wants.

Jenny calls her life up to this point "a waste." Her "problem" is when she takes that small part of her totality and identifies with it. To call her life "a waste" is to reduce it into a fragment.

When she identifies with this, she hates herself and life. We talk and find other aspects of her life besides "waste." She is clinging to the belief that without a love partner she has no value. She discriminates more subtly in seeing that this is not always true for her. It feels this way right now and we see that when she latches on to this thought she hates herself. We notice her superego attacks, and she sees that these attacks hurt her and don't reflect her kinder feelings for herself.

Our longing is lively and deeply felt, and somebody in the past may have told us it is "too much" to bear, or somebody in our past couldn't stand it, so we turn it off and we say we "can't stand it" and we go into our head and say, "it's too much. I can't take it anymore. I'm overwhelmed. I can't take care of myself." If we would be still a few moments, experience the sensations in our body that accompany what we are saying, some new aspect of experiencing would come up in us. The story would feel heard and would then pass, and something new and spontaneous would appear. We may have to learn how to lay aside our stories and move back into present awareness of our senses, thoughts, feelings, and energy as they arise over and over fifty or a hundred times a day until it happens naturally. This is the way of not indulging in repetitive negative stories that only hurt our heart, and don't tell us the truth of who we are.

Jenny tells her story of "no relationship" over and over in her mind — what she did wrong, what she didn't get, never will get, had to live without, can't live without. She is imprisoned in this story only in that she identifies with these thoughts and doesn't let them be until they shift. These thoughts are just looking for her compassion. They want to be heard.

A therapist can work with Jenny to bring to her awareness how she acts out her early-life object relationships of rejection. A therapist can explore the repeated patterns of who does what to whom inside her object relations. As we enter the experience here of frustration, and stay present in it, Jenny's innate potentials may send her the strength or compassion or curiosity to bear witness to her experience, as well as the clarity and intelligence to not believe her story to be her totality.

The way out of this pattern of grasping on to thought fragments is for Jenny to see how she is "doing" her own unhappiness when she grasps this belief, gets involved in it, and believes that there is no place of contentment without a partner. As Jenny speaks of her issues, I point out to her in sessions her arising potentials — strength, clarity, openness, staying present, contact with her direct experience, truth, humor, compassion. She then begins to generate more awareness of her arising assets. In this way she can see herself as transforming, and feel positive energy toward herself. These potentials of health emerging in her sessions as she experiences her pain are then noticed by both of us as they arise and as I validate them in words.

As Jenny begins to admit to herself her feelings, a sense of longing for a companion arises. Her potential for staying present to her own longing was often hidden in her childhood. I am working with Jenny over and over to open into her direct experiences in her body so that energy can transform into new possibilities from within and not just intellectual thought fragments. We explore the imprinted pattern of recreating rejecting relationships based on her attachment to early object relationships and her belief that this is what has to happen to her. She sees how she closes off way before she gets rejected in anticipation of this. I point out the obstructions from the past as well as the potentials for health and healing that are emerging in the present in our sessions. In this way there is an ongoing balance created of emerging healing potentials to support the experience of her internal suffering her past wounds. As Jenny opens into letting her pain be, her potential for being more loving toward herself comes to life. It feels safe enough to emerge into her consciousness, for now it can be welcomed by her.

It's not only what you didn't get that is crucial, it's that you haven't discovered what you have right now as your potentials when you stay present. This is the focus of psychotherapy that happens in the context of spiritual practice and principles. You make this discovery of what you actually have by learning to stay present and watch your process unfold until your potentials lost in childhood begin to come forth to support your healing journey into being yourself. They come forth when you respect things as they are, let them be, and trust that this will naturally clear a space in consciousness for new aspects of yourself to emerge. Healing potentials emerge as you start to listen to yourself, give yourself a space to be, create the stillness to hear what's there and stay present. The therapist mirrors the arising of these potentials so the client can experience them enough to digest them.

When we stay open we see the natural emergence of these potentials and how they come up spontaneously. It's like being in front of a window — everything comes and goes effortlessly when we notice what's happening.

Our inner life keeps moving as thought, sensation, direct feeling, vital breath, flow of consciousness, energy held in the embrace of awareness. When we pay attention, we discover that we are always in a flow of movement and unfolding from within. This whole show is impermanent, workable, and unpredictable. The inner flow moves with plentitude.

Our true human nature contains the wisdom of the universe. As we are encouraged to look and listen to where we are now, we move from the realm of personality, where we take on other people's prescriptions for living, to where we can value ourselves and give space to how we see, to what we hear and sense and deeply know. *Giving the experiences we have inside a space to exist and paying attention to them and accepting them is coming to life and healing into being ourselves.* The recognition of the truth of our experiences in the moment and how they naturally self-liberate is what offers us psychological relief no matter what happens to us. Recognizing the experiences and allowing them to be, without manipulation, allows them to shift. Being aware without getting caught up with thinking we are our feelings is wisdom. We are the awareness itself not the temporary feeling states.

Potentials reflect the innate wisdom of the universe within all forms in nature. There is the same wisdom in us as the wisdom of the seed that will grow into a tree when given the right conditions. This is in a person the same seed that will flower into a full human being when heard and seen in its totality, both psychologically and spiritually. This growth is a process of holding more of ourselves in our awareness without judgment. This is a process of coming to life, of waking up to what is happening. The process of facing what is arising in the present is the practice of awareness. *Being aware is the place where spiritual living and psychological living interpenetrate and cannot be separated.* We have everything we need to heal within us. We just haven't known where to look. Awareness is the great healing key, psychological and spiritual. When we connect with what is here and experience it, we naturally flow with a sense of fullness and completion.

What turns this wish for a relationship into a "problem" is that Jenny does not fully experience the longing, the actual sensations of longing for a partner when they come up in her body. Rather, she thinks it tells a story where she can't get what she wants, and she makes up an ending to the story where she is lonely and terrified for the rest of her life. This ending scares her for there is no opening into anything new in it. She walks around compulsively thinking, *That's who I am, I'm the one who doesn't get to have a relationship like all the other people. I'm the one who can't get what she needs, and I never will. This is because I'm so angry and can't get over it.* With this dismal ending to her own story, she's miserable. True understanding will come when she sees that she is creating her own unhappiness and she will feel there is something more interesting in life than her acting out and grasping her parents' or family's version of her.

The healing for this entire mental construction is for Jenny to begin to feel the anger when it arises in her body, stay present for the pain of hurt underneath the anger, feel the hurt, give it a space to exist, get to know the movement of energy inside the bodily sensations of anger and send compassion into her pain. As she stays present in it and leaves it as it is, the potential for compassion for herself might open as she recognizes and allows her actual sensate pain and stops clinging to her concepts around it. She can then understand the causes and conditions that are its present triggers, see what past transferences are in it of who did what to whom, and notice it shift as she commits to staying present and open in it without acting out her usual patterns of withdrawal and self-attack. New potential for inner support will arise as she stays aware of her anger and lets it unfold. It will take her to places of experiencing memories or sensate bodily sensations around the original wounds which, when felt, will free more of her hidden potentials for being fully who she is. As Pema Chödrön says in *Start Where You Are,* "When you feel that something is wrong, let the story line go and touch in on what's underneath. You may notice that when you let the words go, when you stop talking to yourself, there is something felt and that something tends to be very soft."[1]

੭ ੭ ੭

There was a time in life when I couldn't make a go of my marriage, with all I knew, with all my understanding myself for years in analysis. I couldn't find a way with my mind or my heart to make things work. In my story about my life, I didn't actually get into this depth of pain and I couldn't bear to see the spillover affecting my children. In separating and filing for divorce, with my therapist dead a short time, with two hurt, angry adolescents, I felt ashamed of the depth of my confusion and sense of helplessness. I often moved into my head where I could brilliantly and tortuously obsess and attack myself for my failure. Having practiced Zen meditation for two years, one night I went to hear Maezumi Roshi from L.A. Zen Center speak on "Much Ado About Nothing." He spoke of the inherent freedom, bliss, and peace, within us as we learned to disidentify with our clinging to our mental activity. He quoted the Buddha as saying "The mind in its natural state is radiant and pure."[2] Our natural state, he said, is outside our conditioned patterns of thinking and feeling. He spoke of the mind being free of opinions and judgments at a subtler, quieter level and being purely present in peace and love if we don't interfere with it, if we let ourselves be. He spoke of a clear, open, peaceful, radiant, awake, cognizant, blissful space within us and called it awareness. The pure, naked, awareness inside our mind he called our "true nature," our "Buddha Nature." I had no idea what his words would be like to live, but I had had glimpses of this in my own meditation and had easily forgotten its importance in the distractions and tortures of my everyday living. I was identified with blaming thoughts and couldn't imagine an inherent place of openness, peace and bliss within me.

Finding my true nature within that which Roshi spoke of sounded like the only path left for me to pursue at the time. My analysis, although helpful, had left me attached to the content of my consciousness. I couldn't find a safe home base inside myself that wasn't caught in judgment or opinion.

I didn't know Maezumi Roshi, but went up to him after the talk and asked if I could go out and sit with his Buddhist group in L.A. for two weeks. He was friendly, and said, "That would be fine." His kind tone brought tears. Loving-kindness for myself came up in a spontaneous flash as it does when we're with someone fully present, kind, and open. Something in me said "Yes. Now. Go." In that moment of facing my despair and not knowing what to do, my potentials for intuition and intelligence came forth spontaneously to support me. I had followed them to the lecture and now followed my heart in deciding to go to L.A. In our brief meeting I felt there was an immediacy of presence that took me out of thinking I was at fault.

At that time in my life, my trust in the power of intuition outshone my usual doubting thoughts that said, "You know all this is bullshit for you," or "You know you won't get it!" Part of the difficulty I was having with my pain was my usual reified superego blaming myself for not being able to make things work the way I thought they should. Part of my suffering was the growing pains of breaking open some old ideas of who I was and how my life was supposed to go.

I always thought that if I tried hard enough, figured it out, manipulated the right people, gave up my truth or submitted to others, then things would work out. I had already stretched outside my family viewfinder in finding a relationship and staying in it for twenty years. My image of a mother taking care of her children was cracking apart and opening me into not knowing how to go on with my life.

At the time I certainly didn't believe in the Buddhist prayer that confusion could "dawn as wisdom,"[3] but again somewhere in me I knew it was true. I didn't then know my Spirit would bring forth naturally the potentials in me to heal when I let myself be instead of pushing to change. I wouldn't let myself value what I already knew — that my wakefulness in Right Now would heal my suffering.

❧   ❧   ❧

I was put into a small room in the zendo in L.A., next to the meditation hall. It was too small for a bed. It had a single futon and a couple of shelves for my things. I had come out to California five days after I spoke with Roshi. I went in to meditate in the zendo and soon found that I couldn't control the sobs coming forth. I spoke to Maezumi Roshi about this. I don't remember what he said, except that it felt as though he understood me without words. He was still and received my grief and fear. He gave me permission to go ahead and experience what was unfolding. He sent me to a smaller zendo for beginning students after a few days and said it was great to cry in there since the students were working on koans and the sounds were common. He conveyed somehow that I was okay with my sobbing, and that my life was worth struggling with. He did this in the way he was natural and open with my grief. He did not attempt to fix it or relieve it. He gave me a big open space to be myself, as Shunryu Suzuki advocates in *Zen Mind, Beginners Mind*.[4] The space he gave, I see now, was from his vast, spacious open awareness where my sobs didn't disturb anything. He was bearing witness to my pain, conveying in his presence that he had walked in my moccasins, so he was intimate with grief. In this, there was no attempt to figure out or change but to be kind in the pain. It was natural to my true humanness at that moment that I was breaking apart and falling to pieces. He conveyed that there was something utterly human in not knowing how life is supposed to go and opening ourselves to living it frame by frame.

For two weeks I sat in meditation with myself many hours, usually six hours a day. I cried much of the day, but it wasn't only about what I couldn't do, or how terrible a woman, or mother, I was. I was able to be with myself with some cracking through of heartfelt gladness for my struggle to be true to myself. After a week or so, I noticed the light coming in through the window at dawn and at evening saw the darkness gathering. I began to feel a glimmer of tenderness for the one inside me so covered over with ideas, books, degrees, and theories about life.

So much fear and heartache arose from the love inside me not being welcomed over the years. This was the first time since the birth of my children, since dancing as a child, that I was glad to be me. I knew then that my life was never going to be the way I thought it would. I knew then that these were the tears many women cry when they have to surrender their concepts that they can make it okay for their children. There were tears of outrage, the rage that my life didn't go the way I wanted, that I couldn't get what I wanted as a family. I asked God for forgiveness and begged for no further punishment for my children. One day when for a few moments I was open and aware, I knew that Buddha was my love in my struggle to find the truth. I began to hear other sounds in the zendo and hear other tears besides my own.

In our meetings Roshi told me I was doing good work, being right in the moment and seeing clearly what was coming up, allowing it to happen. I hadn't heard this kind of support in years. I was beginning to open into an intimacy with where I was. This home inside of me took me over forty years to surrender into. Finally, I lived, "Thy will be done." I began to see what I had hidden my whole life — my terror, and sorrow, my strength, and love.

One day there was a moment's joy or pure openness. I found a few moment's space of naked awareness, without concepts. One instant of total awareness. I then knew with certainty I was good as I was, that this was the only place I could be in right now. I saw with compassion that this was the only way I could do this or that "it" could happen. All I could do was be who I was, moment after moment, and "I" wasn't in charge of how that was. With great relief I gave up trying and was still. These were moments of bliss, peace, and openness as Roshi had spoken about in his talk. I had come home.

I would go into the interview room to see Roshi. Once I mentioned my practice was crying and seeing light. I remember thinking that I had come into the world in this state, crying and seeing light, and that I was being reborn into that same light and breath. Light and life force and breath that bring us in and re-create us. I remembered one of my favorite books, *I Am That* by Nisargadatta Maharaj,[5] that spoke of staying present to simply "I am" before I was a mother, wife, woman, therapist, daughter, and so on. Who was "I" really before all these self-concepts? I would imagine Nisargadatta in his loft space fiercely asking people to meditate on who they were before the birth of consciousness as an "I" that created a separate entity. I remembered my love for the question "Who am I?" and for the Zen koan "Show me your face before 'you' were born." I recalled many times "The kingdom of God is within" and realized this "I" that I called "me" would have to be the kingdom of God. I saw clearly that awareness and love are the same thing. In the silence of Zen practice, my life was transforming. All "I" had to do was get out of the way. I stopped chasing elephants outside and rested my weary mind. I let things be. Everything shifted naturally.

On the cushion I sat facing a wall, looking down at a wooden floor where the light from the window danced. At one moment I saw fleetingly that I had to deal with this pain whether I liked it or not. At another moment I saw that I wasn't in charge. I saw that in the bigger picture things happen as they are meant to happen, if I leave it as it is "it" will take care of itself, and shift.

The highest potential was the light coming in the window, my breath, the life within me. The miracle was simply, "Here I am," "I am here."

Although I was a psychologist and trained therapist, I thought I could control the whole show at the same time I thought I was inept and pathetic. I laughed to see that I couldn't fathom any of it. Life was too big to hold in concepts.

At that time in my life, I knew I needed someone to help me who had faith in something inside me that would allow me to heal. At that time, I needed someone who knew what my true human nature was and that my potentials were there underneath my pain to support me. I needed someone to know that happiness was my a priori condition or "always already state," as Da Free John calls it.[6] I needed someone to understand that no matter what life brings there is an innate, unstained healing space within me that was untouched by my past.

At that time of grief over divorce, I gave myself a space and time to stay with what was happening in me, to leave it as it was, and to connect with my own experience. From this I found a love inside me, and it transformed the rest of my life. Coming into the now, in hearing, seeing, being my awareness, was the place from which I could always find a new beginning. It was a place from which I could witness all of my upsets without thinking they were who I was. Awareness became a place for me to hold it all, with gratitude. I could be aware and not cling on to ideas of me. Where I was aware I was free to see what would happen next.

The word *problem* literally means "a difficult question proposed for solution: a riddle."

Inherent in a problem is a question regarding how we are living our life or a question that is "difficult." When it comes to our psychological problems we don't trust that if we are quiet and stay present, our truth of the moment coming through us will inform us of what is appropriate to do. This action of the moment comes out of our inner wisdom and clarity when we are willing to turn toward ourself and go within. According to Buddhism, the very nature of our mind in its natural state is wisdom and compassion.[7]

We learned to forget our potentials. We learned to forget how things are always coming forth from the openness within us, the vital, essential spirit inside of us. In this space our open pure naked awareness embraces everything that life brings us with love and equality. The functioning of the totality and our part in it can only be to respect what manifests in its uniqueness. And to enjoy the whole display as one enjoys each float in the Easter parade, each float unique.

Problems are actually sensations of energy in the body passing through us to which we then attach solid thought forms. They are moving thoughts reified into images and conclusions, opinions, and identities. Each emotion we have is composed of a collection of sensations in the front part of the body from the throat down to the genitals where we sense and feel. These sensations move and flow as energy or pulsations, as a continuum of sensations, vibrations, frequencies, flows, openings and closings, movements, and streamings that never stop until we die. Think of the energy it takes us to keep believing we are stuck.

A natural flow of consciousness would bring us new healthy potentials if we could leave things as they are and trust the natural flow of life to bring us *sat, chit, and ananda,* or existence, consciousness, and bliss."[8]

We often live at a solidified, thought-centered level of the secure and the predictable all constricted in the viewfinder of our parents' view of life. Lama Surya Das, a Buddhist Dzogchen teacher I have studied with, says, "We are in the construction business. We have to get out of the construction business."[9] There's almost no contact with what is actually happening at any moment in all this fabricating.

Da Free John, an American spiritual teacher, said:

> The incident of true understanding is when you observe that you are doing our own limitations and/or neurosis. You yourself are the activity; only you create limitations.[10]

We convince ourselves there is someone else who can help us get over our problems or suffering: maybe a psychic, lover, hypnotist, therapist, guru, coach, best friend, imagist, daughter, son, body worker, husband. We maintain the illusion that we are not quite grown up and will be saved by some wise outside authority who takes the time and sees more clearly than we do, since we don't take the time to stay present and listen or meditate or inquire into what is going on inside of us.

If you had the choice of all the wealth in the world or your conscious presence without which the body would be a cadaver, which would you choose? We often opt to choose the wealth of the world. We do not believe that sitting still and meditating ten minutes on our questions will bring us spontaneous answers from within. If we could be still, and be aware, we would find appropriate answers for right now to our questions. Reflection and meditation open us to the highest potential of intuitive knowing. We prefer to run around and be confused and pay others to tell us what we already know and won't let ourselves hear.

As a psychotherapist, I observe that most people believe it would be a waste of time to bring their awareness to their thoughts, feelings or sensations when they are hurting, to recognize and stay present with what is there, honor it, and learn that it will pass and shift. Our feelings just want us to be there for them, to have compassion for them. Such is the respect our mothers and fathers taught us for what is inside of us. Such was the value we learned to give to our inside life. Such was the value we were taught to give to our presence, essence, being, spirit, soul, true nature as children in our family. The entire miracle of consciousness is overlooked by us. We look elsewhere for answers or we don't question what we are doing to ourselves in running to "fill the holes"[11] within us. There is no way to convey in words the lengths to which we go to avoid being with our senses and feelings and thoughts as they are in process within us—as if life were happening in St. Elsewhere.

Finally there might be an illness, a death, a loss in our life that brings us to our moment-to-moment living, when we can't be in charge or find solutions. We are then brought a blessing in disguise, for life is showing us the way to go inside ourselves, teaching us "to come home," to finally open into just being, to what is present in our body as sensation, thinking, and feelings. This awareness is the entrance the poet Rumi says is "the way of love."[12]

Let's say I'm hurting. We truly needed as children to say to someone, "Please hold me, listen to me, hear what I'm going through, just be with me, stay with me. Let me be as I am." We often learned not to express these needs to our mother or father or anyone. This is what our body and mind need to acknowledge when there is a problem or pain in life. This is what we need to give to ourself.

One Buddhist definition of enlightenment is "a total openness which is indescribable," a "totally open and naked awareness."[13] In meditation and spiritual practice we see through and loosen up a head full of frozen-solid stories that are reified as if they were all there is. We come to realize in spiritual work that all the arisings in us are the Tao or enlightenment manifesting as spontaneous arisings from the source in the universe — the mother of the Buddhas within us. Our awareness holds *all* there is as equal. In Buddhist practice we can come to experience that the entire universe is our true body and we are at one with all forms in nature. We are the unity in diversity, the diversity that includes the totality.

The more we empty our conditioned concepts, the more we are full and can be intimate with more forms in the universe without being upset, for there is more space in our awareness. Joko Beck, a Buddhist teacher, calls this opening of our awareness becoming a "bigger container," and she refers to holding more and more in awareness without being upset."[14] As I see it, this widening the circle of awareness and compassion is our healing journey, both psychological and spiritual. Pema Chödrön in her teaching conveys that we can continue to widen the circle of compassion until we die.

If you stop listening to your inner experience when you have a problem, you are acting out being your mother, you are living the lie somebody taught you about pain: "This is too much; I can't handle it," or some equivalent. I was taught, "You make me crazy. You're too much. I don't have time for this." On top of the radiant, precious being I was, my mother pasted these ideas. I hung on to them for forty-odd years. I really believed I was "too much" for this earth plane. Holding this "too much" thought in awareness as one of billions arising and passing each day is quite different from believing it is the holy truth.

       ર   ર   ર

No problem lasts. Everything is changing and in flux arising from a radiant open space of Mother Universe that the Buddhists call Prajna, the eternal space of origin in which we are "not born, not destroyed, not stained, not pure, neither waxing nor waning"[15] according to Buddhist wisdom teachings. If a therapist does not have a spiritual practice, or has not experienced the nature of mind,[16] which is the self-liberating nature of all that arises, they have not experienced the natural healing power of the unconditioned aspect of the mind. They might see in their clients what is stuck and unhealthy and developmentally deficient. This view of human nature is not natural and reflects a lack of experience with the nature of all things spiritual. Such a view of people pulls them down and doesn't reflect what is dynamically functioning within as our unconfined, ever-healed potentials untouched by our past.

Some of us, without a spiritual practice or context, may not understand that continuing to go over the conditioned dualistic habitual content of the discursive mind is the very root and maintenance of our suffering. Identifying with contents only fires forth more contents. Can the mind heal itself at the content level? Therapy based on psychoanalytic theory has little room for being, for bodily experience, vital essence, or the spontaneous arising of potential for generating health and healing. Healing potentials don't emerge if we only recycle new identifications with mental activity that replays conditioned ideas about what life is. The mind cannot heal itself by identifying with concepts from the past. These have no energy or immediacy, thus they are not real. We can't keep talking about our life and expect anything new to emerge for our ego doesn't know how to find our inner truth, nor does it want to. Ego tries to maintain the status quo, and cannot genuinely move into the unknown. It takes a few moments of stillness, a turning inward, a commitment to giving attention to inner experience in order to discover something new within.

What happens if we sit down with ourselves for ten minutes to contemplate a problem in our life? This is extremely helpful to do. What will we begin to notice in the front part of the body? We might notice a hardness, tightness, pressure in the chest. We go right back up into our head and talk about what we did, what he said, I said. We move out of the body into the head in a few seconds and begin to construct what to do, what happened, the future, the plans, the right moves. We are afraid there is nothing we can do about it anyway. "What am I supposed to do? I hear: 'Leave my husband, walk out on my children, find another job, get into a loving relationship, make more money, be honest.' Well, I can't." The perception of people often is that there is nothing they can do about many of their life problems. "Of course he doesn't love me, desire me...look at me, who would?" "That bastard is an idiot and offers me nothing, but I can't leave the children." "I don't have any idea what to do, I am paralyzed with fear, frozen, confused."I wouldn't be here if there was something I could do, would I?" At times of difficulty if another person will be with us in open awareness for a few moments and listen and care and hear what we are going through, then we might cry or scream, or lie motionless until something new breaks, comes up in us; and it always will.

The difference between feeling broken and whole is our acceptance. We begin to digest and value our own view of things as we are heard/seen in the open awareness of a person who lets us be as we are, and has faith that we already have inside what we need to heal, which will come forth as we turn inward and listen.

At the "bottom of the mind," as the Buddhist scholar Edward Conze[17] calls it, lie our potentials in seed form. We see them spontaneously manifest in meditation practices. These potentials and innate aspects of our true nature are always there within us, in different combinations. Their particular com-bination and emergence is one of the things that make us completely unique; their existence is what unifies us all as human beings capable of being aware of things as they are, capable of being awake and fully human, capable of choosing and creating a life anew at every moment.

The personality ego level of the conditional discursive mind is often unnaturally patterned, imprinted, closed, conditioned, dualistic, attached, repetitive, self-involved, clinging, fixed, habitual, and structured. The healing potentials balance the grasped structures of the mind in the polarity of all of nature. In healing from our spiritual true human nature, we all have both neurotic structures and potentials for transformation and healing within us. In our true nature is the inborn awareness that allows us to come into the now to see what is happening and to start all over again time after time.

As we are held in the arms of a loving person in our early years, so we learn to hold in our awareness the human pains we all come to with loving-kindness. H.W.L. Poonja, a Vedantic Hindu spiritual teacher, said, "If you keep quiet, for just a few minutes out of your entire span of life, perhaps you will win peace. Very few will keep quiet for even five minutes. Instead they go to the Himalayas, they go to the temples. But very few spend five minutes in their house keeping quiet."[18]

When someone is opening a space for healing they bring us to direct experience, to awareness in the moment, to unfolding process as direct experience as well as to the self concepts and thoughts in the mind that obstruct this natural flow. The structures of the mind imprison our deepest potentials. The greatest structures are superego, early object relations, and self-images from the past.

As we stay present, we discover that our true nature, our natural state, is flow. The sense of life then becomes a process. Everything in the universe is in our awareness. We can be clear and intimate with it, for it is within our consciousness. Our sense of self is a process.

We might start talking about some issue where we are hurt, there is solidified thinking, explanations, figuring out, wanting solutions, blaming; then after a few minutes if we stay with our bodily experience we might move, for example, into sadness. Depending on circumstances, we might move into different kinds and degrees of sadness in different parts of our body. Depending on what place we are in right now, we might cry or be silent and respect that sadness, and we can clearly see the causes and conditions that create it. We may see that we have hated or disliked it, avoided it, and not given it much space to exist in our life. *An experience must have space and time to exist in our awareness in order to pass. As any experience passes and we are aware, we are resting in openness, ready for the new event in us to arise.*

In speaking of the happiness of the ordinary when we are in unity, absent our usual separations into "me" and "you," Rilke says in the ninth of the Duino Elegies:

> Praise this world to the angel, not the unsayable one, you can't impress him with glorious emotion; in the universe where he feels more powerfully, you are a novice. So show him something simple which formed over generations, lives as our own, near our hand and within our gaze. Tell him of Things. He will stand astonished...[19]

As we begin to see, to hear, to make contact, we "stand astonished" by the uniqueness, preciousness, and beauty of each and every "thing" our eye falls upon. As we begin to lose the grasping clutch of our ego, as life softens or humbles us, we let go of one image after another, one identity or concept after another, one judgment after another. And finally we just are...

Then we begin again to see, and find the essence of who we are that we have missed. This seeing of ordinary everyday "things" as glorious is what has been missing when we have been lost in our self concepts.

Over and over life teaches us that if we stop distracting ourselves and running away, there is a peaceful and loving place to come home to inside of us, just being ourself, Just Being.

Spiritual experience reveals to us that *we* are the fullness we are seeking. This is it! We are, when fully present, the peace and love we have been looking for on the outside. There is then a disappearance of the interpretation of the object... There is no "one" seeing and no sense of "object" seen, just pure seeing happening.

When we have a problem and we seek help, we hope that the person isn't going to get stuck seeing us only at the level of what is wrong with us. If we didn't have within us the force of life, the dance of consciousness with its vast potentials, if we didn't have the essence of the Buddha from deep within, how would we ever heal into the full, alive, awake, wise human we truly are? A person who has experienced potentials coming forth can help us recognize our own potentials as they emerge and encourage their growth throughout our path of awakening. If we don't see these potentials coming forth from our intrinsic True Nature, we may bog down in the personality and pain, where there is always something wrong with us. Buddhism teaches us that whatever is conditioned creates sorrow. All minds have stories. The issue is that the mind solidifies around the stories and dwells on them for so many years and identifies them as who we are. We can learn that we are pure awareness that holds it all. We can learn how full and peaceful it is to let everything happen on its own and to let go of thinking you are the doer and in control of what happens.

Jack Kornfield, a Vispassana Buddhist teacher, described on one of his tapes called *Taking the One Seat*, about how a flower blossoms and opens:

> That what arises for us is
> Just the next petal of the flower
> That has to arise and open for us
> To be free...[20]

It takes readiness and openness to trust the innate, intelligent flow of life bringing to us the support and guidance that we need in our life journey. Sometimes we need a guide to help us tap into this intelligent flow and encourage us to stay present. One form of guide for this is a therapist who works within a psychological-spiritual context.

The body is starting to come into greater focus in psychotherapy. There are now more body-centered therapies, more therapies that integrate healing in one from or another. I have studied a form therapeutic touch called Polarity, which I use with certain clients who have difficulty speaking. People, when they have problems, sometimes know that unless they get into their body experience and out of their heads they won't feel different, or get out of their conceptualizing. Psychological issues are never over. Nor do they come to an end unless we choose to pop out of our stories when they hypnotize or hurt us.

Unless you actually feel in your body what you experience, you may never digest what you say. Meditation grounds a person in their body. Buddhist meditation often starts with a focus on the breath, asks us not to elaborate or obsess, but to come back to the breath if we do. An instruction in beginning Zen Buddhist meditation is to focus on the breath, and return to the breath as the mind wanders and gets distracted, bringing it back to the vital breath within us which brings us life without our even trying for it. We take for granted these vital human aspects of breath, being, consciousness, awareness, energy, seeing , hearing, tasting, touching, and smelling.

It is a difficult aspect of some kinds of therapy that it puts us into the isolation of being on a couch with a relative stranger who asks us to speak from our head, which is what we do all the time anyway, which is what made us ill in the first place. It is a repetition of feeling so separate and isolated from the person in the room with us whom we called mom or dad. In the room with the stranger-therapist revealing the content of consciousness, it is extremely difficult to contact anything fresh and creative spontaneously arising in us. Can this mind that is identified with content, that is conditioned and based on the view of separation of head from heart, mind from body, person from person, ever heal itself? I don't think it is possible for healing to occur until the energy arising in the body is experienced, until our emerging potentials are brought into the work, until awareness of the process unfolding in the here and now is the focal point, and unless the relationship and the state of the therapist's presence is seen as real not transference.

The most essential aspects in us that humanize and heal us, that bring us our health, have not been mentioned to psychotherapists. Our spirit, our being, our presence, our love, our compassion, our wisdom and faith, our healing potentials, our unstained awareness untouched by the past, have not been taught in therapy training. The natural way human potentials emerge to support us has not been taught in most therapy training programs because we learn of them in spiritual work and the translation to therapy has not often been made. So many therapies have foundered on the rocks of what is the matter instead of recognizing and appreciating what is here right now.

Nisargadatta Maharaj, whom I have mentioned, died in 1981. He inspired many spiritual people to work with the question "Who am I?" He taught many how to work with that question in meditation. As all great Vedantic teachers, he urged us to go into the beginning of our awareness and to experience who we really are before we were trained to believe by parents I am "this" or "that." Nisargadatta Maharaj asked us to simply be, prior to all our concepts, and see what unfolds from that place. Not surprisingly it is often peace and contentment.

In the front part of the body from the throat to the bottom of the root chakra, we have conscious experience of energetic movements. Those subtle energetic movements we call feelings. Sometimes we don't want to experience these feelings, so we constrict the front of the body and move up into our head. It is the central escape route we use to hide from dealing directly with any psychological pain. We use the muscles of the body to contract when we are hurt and then we move up into our head and create and cling to mental content of early-life, object relationships, and act out our patterns that are imprinted within these early relationships.

These bodily close-downs from early relationships that we hold on to in our mind also keep us from taking in interpersonal exchanges with others. When we are sitting with ourselves and have a problem, when we are in some kind of pain, we might notice some of the energetic movements or sensations arising in the chest, or throat, or solar plexus, pelvis, stomach, genitals, or head. We then have the choice to come to those movements and be with them, or to follow our fantasies, projecting our stories and beliefs, judging ourselves, instead of opening to our experiences directly.

In our culture, we have a habit of regarding the physical body as something to be worked on, kept in shape; we regard it as our shell, our persona. We identify it as who we are and want to make it into a more attractive shell. It is often seen as a subsidiary of the mind. When the conditioned mind begins to notice something "dangerous" going on in the body such as sadness, excitement, longing, anger, fear, loneliness, joy, creativity, power, and so on, it closes down and creates a shell of protection to stop something from occurring, making up an argument that what is happening is good, bad, right, or wrong, and so forth.

It becomes clear that no real change in internal subjective experience can be made until the physical sensations in the body are noticed. By being aware in the body, you enter into a give-and-take with the world so that you are nurtured. This is why systems that focus on felt shifts in the body like Eugene Gendlin's focusing are helpful.[21] If we attempted to close down on our breathing, it would be a life-threatening situation, but this is exactly what we do with our feelings and sensations when we attempt to stay up in our head and exclude the feelings or bodily sensations in our experience. Most of our problems can't be solved on a cerebral level. We need the vital force of our bodily sensations to inform us of where we actually are inside at that moment. In this bodily sensed way we know that a basic trust can exist within us. We know, through our body, our experience in the moment. It is from this biospiritual experiential knowing that we actually heal. It is through our bodily felt experience that we begin to first notice where the elephant actually is.

୬   ୬   ୬

Endnotes

1. Pema Chödrön, *Start Where You Are* (Boston, MA: Shambhla Publications, 1994), p. 52.

2. Maezumi Roshi, Public talk, New York City, 1980.

3. Dudjom Tersar Ngondro, *Ngondro Practice* (New York: Yeshe Melong, 1992).

4. Shunryu Suzuki, *Zen Mind, Beginners Mind,* (New York: Weatherhill, Inc., 1997).

5. Nisargadatta Maharaj, *I Am That* (Durham, NC: Acorn Press, 1992), p. 1.

6. Da Free John, Home Study Course.

7. Nyoshul Khengo, *Natural Great Perfection*, trans. Lama Surga Das (Ithaca, NY: Snow Lion Publications, 1995), p. 46.

8. Swami Dayanda, Arsha Ashram, Saylorsville, PA. Talk on Vedanta, October 1989.

9. Surya Das, Guided Meditation, Dzogchen Retreat, Canadaigua, NY, summer 1994, 1995, and 1996.

10. Da Free John, *The Holy Jumping Off Place* (San Rafael, CA: The Dawn Horse Press, 1986), p. 123.

11. A. H. Almaas, *Diamond HeartBook I,* (Berkeley, CA: Diamond Books, 1993), p. 17.

12. Rumi, *Birdsong, 53 Short Poems,* translated by Coleman Barks, (Athens, GA: Maypop, 1993), p. 13.

13. Notes from a summer retreat with Lama Surya Das, Canadaigua, NY, 1997.

14. Charlotte Joko Beck, *Everyday Zen,* (San Francisco: Harper 1989), p. 50.

15. Heart Sutra, translation by Roshi Bernard Tetsugan Glassman and Peter Muryo Mathiesson, (New York: Zen Center of New York, Sutra Book, 1985).

16. Nyoshul Khenpo, *Natural Great Perfection*, (Ithaca, NY: Snow Lion Publications, 1995), p. 71.

17. Edward Conze, *Buddhist Meditation,* (New York: Harper & Row, 1975), pp. 17-18.

18. H.W.L. Poonja, *Wake Up and Roar,* Vol. 2, (Kula Maui, HI: Pacific Center Press, 1993), p. 46.

19. Rainer Maria Rilke, *The Selected Poetry of Rainer Maria Rilke,* Duino Elegy #9, ed. and translated by Stephen Mitchell, (New York: Vintage International, 1989), p. 201.

20. Jack Kornfield, *Taking the One Seat,* (Barre, MA: Audiotape, Dharma Seed Tape Library, no date).

21. Eugene T. Gendlin, Ph.D., *Focusing,* (New York: Bantam Books, 1982).

3

Spirit's Healing Power

People ask me how to get over problems or how to find the support to work with them. What is often creating problems is that our many innate potentials for full life are blocked and obscured by our clinging to the old images or self concepts, thus restricting the spontaneous arising and passing of feelings, thoughts, and sensations. What people call problems are usually the hardened concepts and judgments around uncomfortable energies in the body.

In therapy, we learn to recognize the structures of our minds that repeatedly obstruct our flow of spontaneous lively process. We begin to disidentify with these structures that are blocking the natural arising and passing of whatever is coming up in us. Self-images, identities, ego ideals, superego judgments of how life is supposed to go, block us from the flow of life. Structures in the form of identity with what follows the "I am" — such as, I am a therapist, I am a mother, I am a Buddhist — block us as we cling to them, have to prove them, and have lots of concepts about them. There are structures around our beliefs of how life should go for us, and around who we take ourself to be, and how we see another person. One of the most destructive aspects of the mind is our superego structure, which constantly judges how we are doing based on past scripts that tell us who is better and worse. The superego has structured beliefs about what is right and wrong, including how we should live and how others should treat us. It has ideas that we are supposed to "make" ourself happy. The trouble is that the ways we choose to make ourselves happy are impermanent. The trouble is we are not in charge of how life happens.

At some point in therapy we begin to see the direct relationship between the pain we are in and the way we are clinging to certain thoughts and distracting ourselves from what's happening right now. We are doing it—holding, fixating, believing, acting out. We see how we are choosing to be unhappy by clinging to negative beliefs and old parental training programs of how we are not good enough.

The practice in therapy is to learn to let the pain be when we have it, to breathe into the energy even when we're hurting, to learn to be aware of it instead of hiding from it or abandoning ourself in it. *Therapy teaches people to show up in **immediacy** and to correct the past programs by living in whatever now the present moment offers.*

As we let our pain be, instead of fighting pain, distracting from it, or hating it, it begins to soften and ease and transform. We see that there might be something more interesting to us than the pain, but we have to go through the pain to get to it. We want something else more than we want the pain to be the stopping point, so we see that we have to go into the pain in order to get to that shift in energy that will reveal something else we want. What we intensely want often requires some pain—such as auditions or writing papers or learning to teach, or trust in a relationship, and so on. In therapy we begin to catch when we contract or get stuck in certain thoughts and situations and start to obsess about our story and feel caught up in it. We simply recognize what we are doing and see it eventually as our choice to come into the Right Now and not get so involved in our thinking mind when it's negative and conditioned. We are learning to allow our experience and to trust where it will take us, which will always be to our innate potentials which empower us.

In spiritual therapy we are encouraged to be aware of exactly where we are in the present, which is the opposite of trying to fix our experience or to change it or to imagine we can control it. We can learn with a spiritual therapist one of the great wisdom teachings of Buddhism, which is that everything is impermanent and in abundant flow when we stay present and open. The new fresh moment arises when we accept where we are, for that very recognition clears a space in consciousness for something new to emerge. It's not that we think in a spiritual context that we can get rid of all of these structures of the mind conditioned by our past but rather that we can touch them from a different place with our awareness and our kindness and openness of heart. As Stephen Levine has taught so many therapists, when we pay attention to what is arising in us with compassion, with openness and mercy, we are healing into our inborn natural wholeness. Our problems are not resolved forever, but we hold the pain from them over and over until we make a place for pain more comfortably, with less lying and fear, with less avoidance. We make a place for it all. Awareness holds it all. We learn to settle into what is there with compassion for ourselves. It's that we have been intimate with pain so long that we no longer fear it.

Our problems and conflicts, our wanting, our longing is gotten rid of in the discursive mind by facing it and letting it tell its story over and over. We can then finally say, "Oh, it's doing its thing again" without getting so involved with it, and taking it to be our only reality. We can then say, "I've been down that road with that story, that negative obsession, and I choose to lay it aside right now. I know it hurts me to dwell on it. I might say instead to myself, "Let me open to the present, check into my breath, bring awareness to my eyes and ears and see what is happening now. Let me come into Right Now and see what is happening. This is my choice now. Let me come into the now and show up for myself, and start fresh from right now on the basis of what I see and hear and experience.'"

It is an extraordinary realization to see that it is only our grasping and clinging to negative thoughts and negative interpretations that keeps us stuck in our problems. The bodily sensations pass; the experience shifts when we let it be; everything that arises is impermanent, thus all psychological issues are moving and workable, self-correcting. *The good thing about the mind is that it can recognize its mistakes.*

We discover a wisdom as we practice meditation: Awareness and love feel like the same thing. In the opening of spacious awareness, which holds our pain kindly, there is often a feeling of love or gratitude coming through as a potential for what we have suffered. *The opening into and staying present exactly where we are in the moment is the very functioning of the love we seek, is the very emerging of the love that will support us in our working on our problems.* This is how love opens inside of us. Love opens naturally and we are taking compassionate care of ourself when we are aware. Relief comes from being exactly where you are.

We don't need to collapse or intellectualize or self-attack when we feel stuck in our structures and stories. We can recognize them as programs from the past and see them, hear them, and have compassion for how they were built out of our need to survive, and the fact that we are doing our best to transcend our attachment to them. Our past defenses were built out of wanting to protect our precious being from feeling the losses of not being seen as we truly are. Our sorrow is that we abandoned our own truth of being ourselves to get what love we could. We can see that certain thoughts cause us more pain than we are willing to have, and so we choose to freely lay them aside and not be so involved with them when we recognize their destructive power. We can begin all over many times each day, choosing to begin all over by coming into the Right Now.

Our true nature or spirit can't be hurt. What we really are can't ever be hurt. It is pure, open, clear, unborn, awareness and is forever unstained. It's just right here. *That's why it works to stay present.* It relieves us to recognize what's happening now and to be more truthful with where we are. Being aware of what is arising as it is moving through us is the only way we ever feel consistently full and complete.

We can't make change happen. If we want it to happen, we have to first see that what we are doing is not working. We have to see this clearly, how we are lying to ourself, for the truth in a situation is not what causes our suffering. It is the lies we tell ourselves and our grasping and clinging and attachment to old self-concepts that causes us to suffer. *To change, we have to get out of the way of the flow with concepts and allow what is there to be seen clearly.* If there is going to be change, it has to come from the truth itself—not what they told us. In order to heal the past wounds the only corrective is seeing what's *real* right now. Based on what is true in immediacy we correct past conditioning. We must come into contact and stay present with what's really happening to heal old wounding. Only by staying present in Now can we get new information.

If we really have an understanding of what we are doing to ourself, we won't do it as much. We keep going over the thought content, and in this way we avoid knowing the truth within us which is arising in this very moment. "Know thyself" is the key to ending our psychological pain.

The potentials we repressed or had to hide around the wounds of childhood will emerge only as we face our wounds. As we face them over and over, it will be evident that our potentials and our being, our wakeful presence, begins naturally to replace our past patterns of being deadened, numb, frozen, agitated or caved in. When we face what's happening, we feel an awake presence that enlivens and gives us faith that life is being lived.

I was having dinner with a man yesterday whose young wife was just diagnosed with ALS disease. He was deeply sad and said that he just couldn't believe that this card had been dealt him. He shook his head and said in disbelief, "Not this card. I can't imagine this one." And that is just how it feels — "Not this card." And for things not to make sense is part of the pain of it. And the injustice is part of it, the outrage, and the confusion. And yet, how can we ever know what cards we are going to be dealt? And no matter what the cards are, no matter what the process is, we all have to learn one step at a time to be with where we are with as much kindness and openness to ourself as we have. As we go along with one thing life has dealt us, many new levels appear that we could never have predicted, and we keep looking into that thing more deeply, more compassionately, more humbly... And it keeps changing, and yet new levels are revealed as our life continues. We don't know how we will change in the midst of how the world rolls out for us, but we know how radically different we are from the person we were five years ago, last year, last week. In the same way our bodies keep changing, so do our thoughts, feelings, and sensations. Thus if we identify and grasp on to our thoughts, sensations, and feelings the life that is right now passes us by.

In being with someone who has a hard life problem, our willingness to face the pain with them and not try to cheer them up is helpful. People in pain are not asking us to prop them up. They are asking us to bear witness to where they are, however they can experience what is happening for them. As Nisargadatta Maharaj said, "Just get rid of the unreal and the real will shine of its own."[1] The real way of our being present in life's tragedies is often more consoling than the problem is a tragedy.

In the Tibetan Buddhist practice of Dzogchen, what we practice, in part, when we meditate is to maintain open spacious awareness. We practice abiding in it. A great spiritual teacher of Dzogchen, Namkhai Norbu, wrote of learning to relax while remaining present in all the infinite manifestations of energy that may arise. He said:

> In the state of presence, which remains the same in relation to thousands of different experiences, whatever arises liberates itself automatically. This is what is meant by 'self liberation... But a practitioner of Dzogchen in the moment of becoming angry, attempts neither to block nor to transform the passion, but observes it without judging it. In this way, the anger will dissolve by itself, as if it had been left in its natural condition, allowing it to liberate of itself... Knowledge of the state of self-liberation is the foundation of the practice of Dzogchen.[2]

There are no innate blockages in us unless we start trying to hang on to something or to push something away or to distract from experiencing what is arising. Eventually we begin to trust the whole process in us as always revealing new possibilities, new angles, and new beginnings as long as we draw breath. We learn in meditation to stay open in the natural flow of consciousness, which always brings us what we need to be full and complete as we are. We practice in meditation staying present and not repressing or indulging in our stories. We practice the same thing in psychotherapy as we learn to explore our own process, and stay present. "The infinite Eternal Presence"[3] that we actually are as Nisargadatta Maharaj puts it, holds all of our experiences equally, openly, impermanently. They are analogous to waves on an ocean, the wave being our daily issues, problems, hopes, and dreams and the ocean our flow of consciousness and our awareness holding everything in the phenomenal world in its vast, loving embrace.

Mental clinging, intellectuation fixation devoid of bodily experience, makes us think we are stuck. We can go over something, dwell on hurtful things that happened to us for thirty, forty, or fifty years. This may not necessarily be in the form of direct thoughts but rather some kind of background mood or backdrop of feeling that we are often holding on to and reliving as beliefs or affective states. We often go over who is not appreciating us, who does not accept us as we want to be accepted, who is rejecting us, forgetting us. These obsessions are our constant companions. Our discursive, habitual dualistic thinking is our addiction to avoiding what's really happening in the Now.

Here is a moving example of a young woman who was not able to stay present at an important moment in her life. She thought she had too much to accomplish. Her fear of contact and staying present kept her away from the love she so longed to express and receive.

I saw a young woman who came from a wealthy, politically active family. Her father had been in the government, her sister had a doctorate, and she was preparing to be a doctor. She had spent several summers in underdeveloped countries working in clinics, and had always thought that she would be a doctor. Katie described her working hard during college and

getting into a prestigious medical school. Her family lived in New York City. She was "all on schedule" until her freshman year in medical school when it was found that her father had pancreatic cancer. Her mother, who never talked about her feelings, went into high gear and treatments were begun. Katie wanted to tell her father, whom she loved very much, her tender feelings. She thought of how she might get into the right moment with her father where she could tell him she loved him, but that time was never there as she saw it. She was afraid to create it. She ran from it.

There was no mention of her father's dying in her family. The focus of her mother and sister was on getting the best treatment, and what to do next, and whether to try surgery or not, or to go to the country or stay in the city. Her mother was more and more busy with "so many things to take care of," and the family decided to move for some months to the country once chemotherapy was finished. Katie got "caught up in the round of events," helped her mother take care of social events in New York City, went to medical school the first year, and began to have "strange feelings" that the teaching doctors were not people but robots, that there was no warmth in the students, that she was "a machine." She had to push even harder to keep her attention on what was happening in class.

In the middle of her freshman year of medical school, Katie went to spend the weekend with her family. She had not discussed her father's illness with him once in six months. There was a forced, strained feeling in the family, and she felt that she had to lie and keep her mother propped up with cheerfulness. The focus of talk that weekend was on returning to the city, and how much better her father was doing.

On Monday morning, Katie carried her bag downstairs before she put it in the trunk of the car to return to school. It was a beautiful clear November morning, full of light and briskness. Katie stopped for a cup of coffee, and her father came down to the kitchen. They chatted a few moments, and Katie said she had to run. Her father looked at her and said "Katie?" She paused a moment, as there was something unusual in his voice. He said "Can you stay a while?" She heard the moment, and felt its depth. Something in her took in the tenderness…and then she pulled out of the moment and went into her head, and said, "I'd love to. I will next time, but I have to get back. I have a test this afternoon, and I didn't study." There was attempted laughter on both their parts. Katie flurried out to the car with her father carrying her bag. He shut the door of the car for her, and they both cheerfully waved good-bye.

Two weeks later he was dead.

Katie cried in my office, and said, "I knew he wanted to talk to me. I just couldn't let it in. I couldn't…be…" Her voice trailed off as she began to sob. "Why couldn't I be there? I do the same thing with men, with my mother, with sex… I can't seem to just be. Maybe my father wanted to say something and that would have been the time…but I couldn't let it happen.

"And now I can't go on lying and pretending that I want to be a doctor…'cause I don't. I can't do the work. I can't concentrate. I know I should 'cause I might want it in five years. But now I want to see my friends, and be with people I know, and go to movies, and paint and draw. I can't believe this is happening to me, I don't give up. I'm not a weak person. But now I can't."

I asked Katie what she was experiencing right now. She said, "I'm sad, really sad. I don't want to…I can't stay in school. I stopped going three weeks ago. One day I was listening and then I couldn't hear the words anymore. I wasn't there. I felt the most terrible sadness come over me. I thought I would die, and I couldn't bring myself back to the class. I wanted to curl up in my bed and speak to my father and have him be there."

Katie began to cry and I sat quietly with her. After a while I asked Katie if she could stay within her own wanting. She said that she would have to leave school. I spoke of that, of her giving herself some space to heal and let herself be free of her inner attacks. I spoke of her wish to have time with her friends, to just let herself be. We spoke of her anger with her mother, and how she thinks she has to take care of her mother now.

I spoke of the potential arising in her to care for herself, and she began to say that she had never done this in her life. She was quiet and said "I missed it." I knew she was referring to the moment her father reached out to her tenderly and asked her to stay awhile. Her habitual pattern of running from being present, from loving openly, sent her from her heart into her head. She could not open into the moment of truth and simply be present in the energy of the moment. This is what she has to learn. This is her essential healing – to be and stay open and receive what is happening. We spoke of this in many ways.

As we talked over the next few months, Katie left school, began having dinner with her friends, bought people birthday cards, went to movies, slept a lot, cried a lot, and began to read spiritual books she had never gotten to before. She struggled with her mother's pain, and established some ground rules for living in her mother's apartment.

Katie had some respect for what she was going through, even though she called herself weak, pathetic, passive, spoiled, and so on. She could see that her pain was connected with how she limited herself from staying present in her experience. She had learned to betray the truth of who she was and she felt angry at this betrayal by her mother, then herself. When she could experience her sadness, she naturally opened into her potentials for strength, compassion, and creativity. She felt herself recognize whatever was arising in the moment. She was more open to her creative impulses to see movies, speak with friends, hang out, draw, read spiritual books, sleep, eat her own cooking, and feel her own love and grief.

A great psychological and spiritual grace is to return home inside our direct experience and value it, contact it and stay present in it. Katie needed a therapist to help her with this, because as soon as she tried it on her own she doubted the value of it, degraded it, and thought it was her failure that she couldn't accomplish what she was supposed to, to become a doctor. She had stepped out of the family program. When I first spoke of her natural need to have some space to grieve her father's death, she said, "Oh..." as if it were something she had never thought of before.

Once she told me that the best way to deal with loss was to keep busy. This was her mother's motto. She then added, "I know my mother is completely unreal." Katie could soon see that dealing with life's losses had nothing to do with distractions. She could respect and honor her need to protect herself from pain also. Compassion, strength, self value, clarity, creativity, as well as truth, love and openness came through as she entered her present and past wounds. These potentials continued to support her in her ongoing process of being herself, AS IS, and accepting where she was.

What is it that keeps us so afraid of loving? At some point life throws all of us into caring for ourself in our pain. There will be unlimited support in us to do this once we can let ourselves be and surrender into what's happening.

There is a Source in us from which our thoughts and feelings and sensations arise. This Source in us is the ever-healed, the untouched, the Source of our beginningless, endless, eternal being. Some call it God, or spirit, essence, presence, holy spirit, Buddha nature, true nature, the unborn, being, mystery, soul, heart, Christ consciousness, unity, mystery, Mother Nature, awareness, Allah, totality, ocean of consciousness, primordial awareness. Some people discover the highest potential within them in Christian prayer, in the Sufi Beloved, in the light of consciousness, or in the pure awareness of the Buddhists. Whatever way we understand the functioning of the highest potential in the universe, we know we have a place inside that contains this potential and is never touched by our past...is always unobstructed and innocent.

Everything that arises speaks to us and moves on. This understanding that we intuitively have that nothing lasts creates insecurity in us. So we begin to cling to certain thoughts to give us a false sense of security. Truth is revealed when we live in the "awareness of nowness."[4]

I sometimes wonder how I can express all the love and energy I feel when I let myself be. I realize many of us are afraid to be free for fear we won't be able to express all that we feel we are. The life within me, as I started to contact it, asked to be lived. If I did not express my loving or creative energy, I began to feel all that I knew was being unlived by me. Better, maybe, to stay asleep. If I see all the beauty arising, and all the intimacy I feel with people and phenomena in front of me, I will have to let go of my attachment to my mother's negative view of me — that there is not enough love in this world for me to get some — and then I will be asked to be present in my life and responsible for my actions. Stephen Levine teaches in his books that the hardest thing we will ever give up is our suffering.[5] This that I haven't yet digested that emerges is the growing edge[6] in me, and the power of it wakes me up. It is out of my hands, I realize. I have tapped into a dynamism that just keeps burning "me" up in my gratitude for life.

I went to see a spiritual teacher, Mother Meera, in Germany several times. I wrote this seeing her the first time:

> Thank you for burning me up, Divine Mother
> Help me remember… Love without end…
> Radiant source
> I accept the invitation…
> And pass it on…
> Life in the furnace
> Force of the heart!

Psychotherapy in this new century will be greatly influenced by Buddhist psychology as I see it. It will focus on the emerging health and resilience and positive potentials of a person as they awaken and learn how to communicate their natural healing power within. It will focus on kindness and positive features, as the Dalai Lama has taught. Psychotherapy will learn how to bring each person's unique potentials to fruition, learn to see them and welcome them, validate them. Psychotherapy will learn to respect and reflect the natural polarity of health and illness in all of nature in its work. Increasingly, as therapists do spiritual work, as their consciousness opens into wakeful presence, they can connect with clients more easily, have more empathy and faith in what their clients have inside as their unconfined capacities to heal. Training will focus on the healing process, and on process itself. Therapists can also learn to respect their clients' willingness to heal or not more easily and let this be.

As Andrew Weil and Deepak Chopra have taught, there is spontaneous healing going on in the body all the time. Spiritual

this. Healing happens as we realize the totality of
who we are and accept that each moment is always the
functioning of totality.

There are some basic conditions, as I see it, necessary to heal.
We must create the inner stillness to listen, and then receive
what arises. We must turn toward ourselves and show up. We
give our experience a space to exist in our awareness, and then
pay attention to what our wisdom reveals of how to act next as
we see clearly what's happening.

The breath is a metaphor for the endless flow of life
naturally coming to us. It brings us what we need to live. We
don't have to manipulate it, fight for it, deserve it, prove
anything to it, produce for it — we don't control it. We just accept
its gift to us. The breath just comes and brings us what we need
to stay alive. The earth holds us in its gravitational field
naturally and the fluids within us bring us nurturance, all
naturally. And within the space of our awareness within lie all
our inner unstained potentials to be a whole, complete, happy,
expressive, loving person. Every moment we can choose to
begin our life fresh. We can choose how to be and act mindfully
for the rest of our life. *It's not what we didn't get that makes us
suffer; it's that we haven't discovered what we have inside. We can
trust our awareness to offer us new possibilities for the rest of our life.*

What is necessary for us to come home and be at ease is a return to our natural flow and to be aware of it, not expecting anything in particular, not knowing what will happen. We are in it already...awareness is everywhere. It is our spontaneous innate healing instrument and we live surrounded in it. It is the root of our spiritual wisdom within and without.

ৰ   ৰ   ৰ

Clients often say they are not really "there" in their lives. It's like the joke "Having a wonderful time...wish I were here." Here's a typical example of a client not being "there."

Alice was telling me she had been attracted to a man the first time she had met him in a meditation group about three months ago. She noticed he was aloof and felt it was difficult to talk with him. She wondered if this was the way he was or if it had to do with her. She asked her girlfriend if he was single or straight, and what sort of person he was. She said she was turned on to him.

She found out from her friend what he did, other women he had been with, and some of his interests. The information seemed to agitate her, especially when she told me he taught philosophy at a prestigious college. She said, "I'm not going to pretend that I come from that kind of background." She sounded equally upset in telling me of his two former lovers, one of whom was a novelist and the other a poet. She laughed, and said, "I have no interest in literature. The only books I read are spiritual. I'm not going to play that game."

The next session she told me she had introduced herself in the social time following meditation. She told me excitedly he was going to call her. She continued to ask me if I thought he was wealthy, saying "I'm not going to pretend anymore that I have money or that I have some fabulous education." Alice said she was glad she had lost some weight, "but if he wants some pretty young thing he better think again. I'm not going to turn myself inside out again about how I look. He probably won't call anyway. If he does there are some games I'm not going to play. I want to get it straight with him I'm not the intellectual type. I don't know how come he thinks I am. Well, I'm not. [Her voice was angry.] I've pretended most of my life and I'm not doing it again. His fancy school and his fancy dames – I come from a blue-collar family...matter of fact, my father was an alcoholic, so if that isn't good enough for him, tough. I want to make it clear to him from the start who I am. I'm not that kind of chic woman he's been with."

Alice continued talking to herself out loud about who she was and wasn't going to be. She told me then that she wanted him to know exactly what kind of spiritual background she had, and that it wasn't the fancy Tibetan kind, but "Just plain Zen."

She is busy "constructing" a reality before much actual interaction takes place. All the talk distracts her from her fear of just being present and open with her own experience with this man. She begins contracting and projecting without speaking to him in anticipation. She is moving into a mood of negativity since "he probably won't call," which attempts to keep her excitement and longing in check. She is angry at him already for not liking her in her argument in her head. She holds the excitement and pleasure as potentials emerging at arm's length. I point them out, along with how she is creating obstructions to being open and not knowing with her stories and fabrications. She is preventing her actual experience from being felt.

As we talk in this session, Alice is getting a bit more down and ends up saying cynically, "Let's see what happens. I know he won't call anyway, but if he does I'm going to be prepared." She is reliving the early-life rejecting object relationship with her mother.

This is a common way we attempt to separate from our genuine inner experience, our excitement, our spontaneous curiosity to meet someone, our sexual needs, our clarity in knowing whom we are drawn to. As we talk I point out her object relations in anticipating rejection, along with her emerging potentials for pleasure, clarity, and curiosity. These innate potentials for more possibilities are being squashed with her gluing to her idea that "no matter what happens, I know what is going to happen."

By the time the phone rings, if it does, Alice will have protected herself by projecting a collection of memories and opinions and conclusions onto a new life situation full of possibilities. All this and it hasn't even taken place.

We help clients disidentify with their negative images and beliefs by recognizing them and seeing that they don't help, they have never helped for they don't represent the truth of who we are. "How come you choose to hold on to your suffering by grasping your negative ideas of yourself?" is a question I will ask Alice. We come to realize a thousand times over how we are holding on to our suffering by grasping our mother's or father's negative ideas of us. As we are aware of this act of holding on it shifts. When we see what we are doing to ourselves we have a choice. We just have to send awareness into our experience. Awareness is the healing agent.

Frame by frame life is lived and choices are made. Just this moment. Now just this. Now this too comes up in awareness. When people say they don't know what to do, they are usually saying they are not present in the moment so they are not receiving messages and signals from what is happening. Without being still and receiving our experiences, we don't know what to do, how to be. *We won't let ourselves know what we already know.* We keep ourselves strangers.

What is going on for us right in our feelings are moment-to-moment clues that want to be noticed and respected and acted upon. Our feelings just want to be heard. When feelings come up, they are asking for compassion and the clarity of awareness. Don't give up on yourself…stay open and present with what arises. Emotions, thoughts and feelings need comfort. Tell them, "I'm here" and soon they go away. There are two friends you have who need your comfort. They are called body and mind. They dissolve when they are heard and respected. If you say that doesn't happen for you, then you are not fully present in Right Now and staying present.

This practice of returning to our present awareness, returning to our bodily experience, valuing our feelings and thoughts is a lifelong spiritual-psychological practice of maintaining connection to Right Now. It can be practiced in psychotherapy, in spiritual meditation, or in daily life. We can catch when we're lost in thought, see how we're clinging to negativity, catch how we're spacing out…then return to our present awareness, to what we hear and see now directly in front of us, to the wakeful sensations in our awareness right now, to our breath, to this very moment. This is a spiritual-psychological awareness practice we can do for the rest of our lives to deal with whatever life brings us. We will have to do it many times each day before we get used to it, before we do it naturally. Lost…come back into the Right Now…over and over. As a client said to me recently, "I fall in love with life over and over when I'm here."

The gift we have been given is that we all have the healing power of awareness to live a fresh, full life. Accept the gift of spirit's healing power — pure vivid awareness, awake and clear, untouched by the past, fresh in the present. Live in this beginner's mind. The elephant you are chasing is at your hearth. Come home!

Endnotes

1. Sri Nisargadatta Maharaj, by Ramesh S. Balsekar, *Pointers From Nisargadatta Maharaj* (Durham, NC: Acorn Press, 1982), p. 106.

2. Namkhai Norbu, *Dzogchen, the Self-Perfected State* (Ithaca, NY: Snow Lion Publications, 1966), pp. 59, 60.

3. Sri Nisargadatta Maharaj, *The Nectar of Immortality,* ed. Robert Powell, Ph.D., (San Diego, CA: Blue Dove Press, 1996), p. 59.

4. Sogyal Rinpoche, *The Tibetan Book of Living and Dying* (New York: Harper Collins Paperback, 1994), p. 44.

5. Stephen Levine, Talks given on healing at Omega Institute, Rhinebeck, NY, Summer 1992.

6. Diane Shainberg, *Healing in Psychotherapy, The Process of Holistic Change* (New York: Gordon and Breach, 1983), p. 34.

Healing Into Awareness and Self-Knowing

This is where the misconception lies: thinking that you are an entity who must achieve something so that you can become like the entity that you think I am! This is the thought which constitutes "bondage," identification with an entity, and nothing, absolutely nothing other than dis-identification will bring about "liberation." (Nisargadatta Maharaj).[1]

Witnessing the discursive mind's madness and programed reactions is not to take it so seriously. Rather we see that everything arises and the major activity that is helpful for well-being is to give it all an equal space to exist, let it be and stay present for the next moment when it self liberates and something new begins.

When you work with people psychologically, what is profound is how diverse people are yet how unified in their wanting to connect with their deeper roots, their own truth. People who come to see me for therapy or counseling often want a "peek" inside. The thought jams we create by clogging up our thoughts around a worry won't give space for anything new to emerge. But the thing that truly consoles and relieves us is finding the truth of exactly where we are right now. Showing up with what is unfolding creates space in our consciousness. What we can do in our life when we show up is to observe our process, let it be, let it shift on its own and act with clarity from seeing what is going on.

People want to change without seeing where they are inside. They have been separated from a sense of home base and grounding. There are usually ideas and fears that nothing will be there inside or horror will be there. This comes out of our early merging experiences with mother or primary caretaker where being the permeable, vulnerable, subtle precious Being we are, with an awareness capable of holding whatever is there, we picked up all our mothers' mood states and feelings. We didn't know the difference between her and us. So we're afraid to see inside. To turn toward ourselves, look within, stay present and open, scares us more than anything in life. I hear people ask me, "What if there is no love?" "What if nothing is in there?" or "I don't care what's inside, I just want to get better." "I'm in so much pain now I can't take any more."

I went into a dress shop recently on a local street. There were three salespeople there. Nobody said hello or greeted me. Two clerks were talking, one staring into space. I went over to the racks and looked awhile. No one made contact with me. I walked out of the store. I saw that I also had not said hello. Why had I been so ungiving?

*"Hello...*Is anyone there? *Hello."*

Why do we give so little in contrast to the vast storehouse of potentials inside us. Our potentials yearn to emerge and express themselves. Why do we contract from relating so often? All these fancy poems and words we use to connect with. Why do we back off from making contact, from giving the love we feel, from being kind? The way we isolate each other is clearly reflective of the way we isolate ourselves. Learning to be present with our own process will break our heart open to our compassion. Our wisdom is seeing things as they are, just as our compassion is the heart-mind response to the beauty and miracle of what is here Right Now, in front of us and in us.

ও   ও   ও

Seeing what is happening inside can be put in so many ways to encourage clients to stay present and value what they see. For example,

"Allow your heart to find its own Truth
whether there is pain in there or not."[2]

"We are here to uncover things. We are not here to
prop each other up."[3]

"An open heart is a much greater gift than illness
is a tragedy."[4]

"Learn to trust the truth of your own experience."[5]

One Buddhist definition of truth says truth is "free from thought, yet everything is vividly known."[6] As we move into dualism in childhood — the "I," "me" and "you" — we move into the story of evaluating and comparing, liking, disliking, and judging. The experience of awakening is to see the true meaning of things. *What is the deep meaning of things? Simply that they exist. This in itself is the miracle.*

Things arises in us naturally and continually like a fountain of life coming from a pure, radiant source within. This unconfined unfolding is what Deepak Chopra calls "pure possibility," which he terms one of the seven spiritual laws in the universe.[7] As we realize how phenomena continue to arise and pass in us until we die, we don't have to identify so much with each particular wave in the ocean. We can observe without identifying. Everything will continue to manifest in our consciousness until our vital breath ceases.

At any moment that we are willing, we can choose freedom. We are always able to make new choices each moment. Each of us is resilient and has the resources of our innate potentials. Dzogchen Buddhism calls reality seen with a sense of pure awareness the "Great Perfection."[8] *Things are perfect when we don't expect them to be any other way than the way they are.* Each moment is perfect when you don't compare it with anything else. The fact that we can be an open listening space for one another is the action of healing.[9] One of the most common experiences people have after a period of silent meditation is gratitude for this precious life and for things as they are. In meditation we have the stillness and space to open our eyes and see the beauty of what is there in front of us. This deep gratitude for the way our clients, friends, family, and lovers are in their diversity requires the stillness to receive this.

A therapist's presence or open awake awareness becomes the container that invites a willingness to go inside. The openness of the therapist's consciousness is one vehicle of healing. This is a space of not-knowing, without opinions and conclusions. Freud and his followers ascribed meanings in therapy and found connections with the past that were helpful. Freud, however, was not aware of spiritual process. When someone respects us as we are and knows the highest innate potentials that are emerging in us, this validates their unfolding, and we begin to value our flow of experience and change our perceptions of what kind of person we are. *The great power of the mind is that it can see its own untruths.* Once seeing these untruths, we can disidentify with them.

Who we are, from a spiritual perspective, is answered in so many ways. We are the light or dance of consciousness, energy, the five elements, the dynamism of the life force, the vital breath, and pure, vast, eternal, unborn, undying, awareness that holds everything in the universe intimately and equally. In a Buddhist view, awareness has room for everything and holds it all with wisdom and compassion. Psychotherapy finds ways to expand our awareness so that we learn to hold more of what we are with zero rejection. For the rest of our lives we can widen the circle of compassion for what life brings us.

❧ ❧ ❧

Getting into inner process work with couples has many possibilities. With couples I often ask them to be present together, for five minutes without words, paying attention openly to what comes up inside of them. Most couples feel the other isn't being there for them much of the time. I ask couples to spend five minutes each saying what they are aware of, what spontaneously arises after being in silence with their partner. Most people are surprised at how easily they tap into what their partner actually feels. I sometimes have a half-hour breath session with a couple and then have them spend time being together, hearing and seeing what comes up for each of them. I have couples do Gene Gendlin's focusing work together.[10] I sometimes ask couples to meditate together in silence on the issue of their relationship and see what spontaneously arises after ten or fifteen minutes. I have also had couples do sensory awareness exercises with each other and see what comes as they are being together.

It is revealing how much longing there is for being seen and heard by their partner and how much fear there is when partners commit to staying present with each other in session. They are afraid of being in contact for fear they can't hide their powerful feelings. People often say how deeply they long for their partner to "be there," and they feel their partner is too distracted to stay present. "You don't really see me, hear me, want to be with me" is what I hear most often. Psychological work for many couples is in seeing what spontaneously unfolds in the immediacy of being present to one another. Inquiring into the fear that being fully present evokes is fruitful. We see how contact in the immediacy of now and staying open feels alive and fresh and stirs longing to be ourselves with our partner.

❧ ❧ ❧

A woman came to see me several months ago. She was studying a psychological process of discreating her beliefs. As she let go of some of these beliefs she had an increasing sense of deadness within. She was disconnected from her bodily sensations and feelings states most of the time, and her beliefs had been her inner hole fillers. This woman was raised by a mother who didn't remember that she had gone home to visit her on a weekend even though she hadn't been home before that for two years. As she began to discreate her negative beliefs in this technique she found nothing of creativity, or peace, or bodily sensation or colors or images moving inside of her. She had learned to freeze the pain of her mother not being present by disconnecting from many of her inner experiences. She clung to the idea that she was dead inside. As I asked her to move inside and to bring her awareness into the front part of her body, in her stomach, she began to notice "tickles" there "as if I am trembling inside." She was surprised to find there was life inside of her, and laughed with relief.

Meditators say, for example, of the intimacy and vastness of their inner experience:

> Something mysteriously formed
> Born before heaven and earth.
> In the silence and the void standing alone and
> unchanging, ever present and in motion. Perhaps it
> is the mother of ten thousand things. I don't know
> its name.
> Call it Tao for lack of a better word,
> I call it great.[11]

People are brought together by a multitude of causes and conditions that allow us to appreciate and honor the karmic complexity of our spontaneous meeting. We couldn't begin to grasp all the amazing circumstances in the universe that have to come together for us to sit and have a session in therapy. Imagine the whole universe. Now imagine how you are brought together with some people in the dance of life, how you are interconnected with some people for brief spans in this vast blazing vital force pouring forth in the endless manifestations we call living. How all this movement is orchestrated is the mystery. "God's will" says it as well as we can grasp it.

The natural way that everything comes up spontaneously from within suggests that there is indeed something being played out in this life bigger than we are able to fathom, in which we are definitely not in charge. Just as we experience the intrinsic intelligence of the way our bodies function, why not trust the intrinsic intelligence within ourselves for knowing, sensing, seeing what feels like the right way to act and be right now?

J. J. Krishnamurti always said, "I am the world."[12] He also said repeatedly that the observer is the observed. When there is no sense of a separate "I," no sense of a separate self-conscious "me," we can feel intimately close to all we see.

Each person we see represents a part of ourself, a part of our totality, and every action reflects the functioning of totality. When we see a person we don't like, we are not accepting a part of our own totality.

When you have pain, when you go into the body sensations of it, put aside the story line, and stay present in it without making up constructs, there is the potential for compassion for yourself to arise. You might own your anger with the people who are treating you badly, and the potential might emerge to value yourself and talk to that person directly. You might stop attacking yourself when you let yourself be and notice your experience. You might feel stronger inside as you face your pain. When you allow your pain to open as experience, you might feel clearer as you see the truth of where you are in the moment and how you can move in a situation. Wherever you are is where you have to start to heal. Staying present and open and not acting out is what is meant by "working" on yourself in therapy. You are willing to sit with your own unfolding process without abandoning yourself. You are willing to stay with your energy as it shifts.

As we hold more and more parts of ourselves with intimate recognition, we can relate to things we see and people we meet with fewer concepts and illusions about how life should be. "Leave it as it is" is a teaching from Dzogchen Buddhism regarding how to experience our natural being with greater wisdom and compassion.[13]

I often ask clients to be still and meditate on their questions such as "Should I do this or that?" and simply be still with their questions and contemplate them for five or ten minutes. Most clients who can remain a few moments in silence find an "answer" or response coming through them to their questions. They want to know if this is the "right" answer. What we know is that it is the right answer in the moment. It is the truth of the moment. As we know, we can only work with where we are just this much, just this moment. We can only work frame by frame.

We have a million ego humiliations and a million spiritual joys when we pay attention to ourselves. Eventually we opt to pay attention to the moving process going on in the present rather than dwelling and obsessing on the voices from the past or projections of the future. One way we change is that life throws us something and we get more interested in that something in the present moment than in our stories and self images.

ए   ए   ए

A woman with arthritis came to see me saying she wouldn't do the exercise or dieting that the doctor told her to do. I did a focusing exercise with her and she came to see that she did many things for others, but taking care of herself didn't make sense to her. She was able to say she had a lot of "sickening" experiences as she contemplated herself "caring for me." Interesting, I said, "that you care for others but are 'sickened' when you contemplate doing that for yourself." Images of people making fun of her, her being a weakling, her needing a wall between herself and others came forth spontaneously as she inquired into "taking care of me." I directed her attention inward and she came to a tightening in her chest. I said she was clear she didn't want to diet or exercise and this is where she is right now. I mentioned the importance of acknowledging this, for it clears a space within for her to feel real with where she actually is when she knows she won't be criticized for it. "We are exploring," I said, "noticing where you are, not judging." I asked her if she could be curious about caring for herself and see what came up.

She told me how good she felt to be honest and began talking of her hopelessness in getting better. We had established a ground within her of being aware of things as they are for now. As she explores within, she is mirrored and encouraged to stay present with what she finds, she will of course open and transform. I have faith in this, for it happens with everyone when they stay aware of their direct experience as it unfolds.

As Pema Chödrön teaches, you always have to "start where you are."[14] It's going to transform no matter what it is.

We have to learn experientially that to stay present with things as they are happening takes *practice*. When we go off into our head, we learn to come back to our body sensations and return to the now of experiencing. Our self-induced trance living can be broken through when we recognize it. Sometimes we spend a whole day dwelling on negative thoughts, attacks of judgment. In whose hands is our life when we identify who we are with the content of consciousness rather than in our Being?

It is from the grounded place of where we are in our body that we start to deal with our psychological issues. There is a distinction between our bodily sensations and our elaborate concepts about the issues. Vulnerability with grounding in our breath, in our belly or chest, or in what we see and hear directly is very different from feeling vulnerable with no grounding in the body. If we are angry we start there, if deadened we start there, to inquire into what is in us as bodily sensations in specific detail. We can always inquire into what's inside us from the place of witnessing, from the place of awareness. Only by going inside our bodily sensations can we learn that pain is temporary when we give it its place to exist. We then see that bodily sensations are where the pain actually is, not in our fixated stories about the pain. It is the stories we tell about the pain that scare us. Under our fixed programmed concepts is always the clear openness of awareness, the open space of the new moment empty of concepts, full of possibilities.

There are examples of people being in psychological pain everywhere we look. Buddha said that life on the relative conditional plain is full of suffering, for nothing lasts and we are separated from our true human nature, which is always there holding our potentials. Having a negative attitude about the pain of our life causes more suffering; resisting pain causes pain to keep building up. As pain arises it just wants us to recognize it, be there for it, hear what it has to say, have compassion for it and it will pass on its own, feeling heard.

A young woman had been seeing me for almost a year. She was often angry that she couldn't find a man. She was in a chronic state of running around doing things, looking for someone to be with, to fall in love with. She was resentful that she didn't have money like some of her friends. Although she went to work, she felt she didn't make enough money. She wanted to write short stories but she felt she couldn't get clear enough to make the work as gripping on paper as she felt it. This frustrated her enormously. She hated having to write after her full-time job instead of when she felt like it. She longed for freedom to write but had never had it. Frustration was her basic life experience. Longing was her identity.

She began a session saying, "It's Tuesday and I don't know what to do when I leave here. I could go home and sit and try to write, but then I get lonely and feel bad 'cause I can't write, I'm too tired. Also, I think I'm isolating myself, I really should go out to meet people. Then I think I'll go out for a while. I could go to a bar. I know some people there, but I don't really meet anyone. They're just looking to get laid, but so am I. Even when I'm having fun, I'm thinking who I might go home with...when I really want to be with Sam. I think of his life with Susie and I feel bad, really lonely, and...I don't know what to do. What am I supposed to do? If I stay home I'm lonely. If I go out I'm lonely. I don't see any way out." Her tone was angry, blaming. "What am I supposed to do?" was an accusation that I hadn't told her what to do. She was angry that she was feeling longing for intimate contact and didn't have it. Instead of acknowledging her anger as a lively potent thing that could open her to her hurt and maybe her compassion for herself, she was fighting her own feelings as if her whole life shouldn't be happening this way. Her "idea" of what a life should be wasn't happening and this angered her. She was not in experiential contact with her own sorrow or loneliness, even though she used the words. She was complaining to me that her life was no good, not the way she thought it should be. She had little kindness toward herself, or ability to stay present in her feelings, or find intimate contact within herself. She looked for love and contact and immediacy only outside herself. She was frantically chasing elephants.

Karen despises her loneliness and won't give it space to exist. She considers it a sign of her failure, rather than how she feels at certain times. She had told herself that her life will continue this way. Karen goes to bars to avoid her pain and misses the man who left her for another woman. She distracts herself from this pain with obsessive planning, intellectualizing and attacking herself.

As our sessions continue we work with the inner attacking tyrants in her superego. She learns how to speak with them and protect herself from identifying with them. This is creating some space in her consciousness to experience her fear and longing. She is pleased at the results of her writing. She is raging at Sam, and her mother, and people who couldn't grasp the person she is. This rage reflects her powerful energy as well as the extent of her hurt at being unseen, unheard by them. As Karen talks of being abandoned, by me for not understanding how it feels to be alone, at God for not giving her money, she experiences her truth as real and vital, and her potentials for strength and clarity and creativity hidden since childhood begin to come forth in sessions. I mention the emergence of those potentials and welcome them. We talk about what blocked her creativity and what obstructed valuing her experience in growing up, and how these are appearing now to support her longing for love and creative expression. By noticing and validating her arising potentials she includes them in her being herself.

Her potential for compassion is coming up as she can be present with her anger and frustration and know that she is not bad for having it. Compassion does not have to do with taking pain away or fixing something, but with being open and willing to see the actuality of one's pain. As she experiences her anger she see that it shifts in its energy. We are not trying to change her pain or get rid of it, but to generate kindness in it.

Karen begins to speak of loneliness and her fear of staying present in it. She is afraid it will always be there. We speak of her difficulty in trusting. She doesn't know what to trust inside of her. We speak of her self-image and how she was taught that loneliness is a shameful thing that is her fault. She would therefore have Sam if she wasn't so "deficient" (her word and distortion). She talks with me, telling me how it hurts to be lonely. She carries loneliness in her chest, but she isn't ready to go inside there and see how it moves as sensation in that wounding in her chest of not being allowed to be herself as a child. She doesn't trust that her sensations will shift if she stays present in them and bring her new potentials to support her healing process. She doesn't trust that she can be in her own truth with me and be welcomed in her unique way of being Karen.

Karen believes that pain is "too much" rather than seeing it as part of her life that will come and go depending on life's causes and conditions. When she looks at who she is, she tells me she is most herself in realizing that she wants to write and will continue to do this. She recently told me, "I am okay, but tortured." She and I both validate and appreciate the appearance of this "okay." This self-value represents a deep change in her inner sense of herself and her willingness to

*leave things as they are and trust the innate wisdom we have to
bring us the potentials we need to heal.*

❧   ❧   ❧

A client said to me recently, "Don't throw me in the garbage,
don't throw me out. I am just garbage." Clients, when going into
their inner process, begin to feel that their parents wanted to
throw them out the window, or in the garbage, or eat them alive.
It feels terrible in the body when we remember this felt sense of
not being seen or known in our lovableness, not even noticed as
we are. The body aches, there are bands of tension everywhere,
the chest caves in, we space out, we are furious for no obvious
reasons, our body trembles, our torso contracts upward, we go
dead, feel raw, can't relax or sleep, can't dream or have orgasms
or know what we feel and think, we are numb or distorting what
is happening. We don't believe love exists anywhere in the
world when no one wants to get to know us as we truly are.
Many pains come up bodily when we remember how no one in
our family was interested to get to know us, or let us be ourself.
Then the mind begins to fragment and think "I can't. This is too
much. I'm no good. I'm not enough." We can't find our new
potentials within ourselves when we don't go into these deep
wounds of childhood. Of course, *we can only enter inside our pain
and care for ourselves when we are willing and when we feel we have
some internal and external support to do this.* Most people feel that
they have never shown the depth of their pain to anyone in their
life including themselves. Clients have told me they are
crippled, badly burned, mutilated, disgusting, repulsive,
poisoned, freaks, dead, vile, and hideous. This is how they walk
around feeling about themselves much of the time. To face pain
is to naturally see it unfold and dissolve and shift into
something new. To face pain when it is there is the only thing
that brings relief. We all yearn to be ourselves in truth, as we are.

Clients know right away the great relief that comes in facing their pain, for they begin a process in pain and end up in a totally different and always good place for having faced it. Pema Chödrön, a Tibetan Buddhist teacher, says of how we start facing our inner life:

> Start where you are. This is very important. Tonglen practice (and all meditation practice) is not about later, when you get it all together and you're this person you really respect. You may be the most violent person in the world…that's a fine place to start. That's a very rich place to start…juicy, smelly. You might be the most depressed person in the world, the most addicted person in the world, the most jealous person in the world. You might think that there are no others on the planet who hate themselves as much as you do. All of that is a good place to start. Just where you are…that's the place to start.[15]

Roshi John Daido Loori, a Buddhist teacher, says:

> There is no escaping the fact that getting beyond this accumulated conditioning is a long process. Thirty or forty years of programming takes time to work through. We look at the thoughts, acknowledge them, let them go, coming back to the breath. Day by day, we uncover what is underneath all of the conditioning. What we discover is called freedom. It is called human life. It is called wisdom and compassion. It's the nature of all things.[16]

A part of what attracts people to Buddhist teachings and practice are its ways of teaching the nature of mind. In the meditation practice you learn to be intimate with how your mind actually works and what relieves its suffering. Sogyal Rinpoche, a Tibetan Buddhist teacher, has written brilliantly and helpfully on the nature of the mind. Here is a quote that distinguishes between our everyday discursive mind and the very nature of mind:

> There are many aspects of the mind, but two stand out. The first is the ordinary mind, called by Tibetans, *sem...Seen from one angle, sem* is flickering, unstable, grasping and endlessly minding others' business, its energy consumed by projecting outward. Yet seen in another way, the ordinary mind has a false, dull stability, a smug and self-productive inertia, a stone-like clam of ingrained habits.
>
> Then there is the very nature of mind, its innermost essence, which is absolutely and always untouched by change or death. At present it is hidden within our own mind, our *sem*, enveloped and obscured by the mental scurry of our thoughts and emotions. Just as clouds can be shifted by a strong gust of wind to reveal the shining sun, and wide-open sky, so, under certain circumstances, some inspiration may uncover for us glimpses of this nature of mind. This is because the nature of mind is the very root itself of understanding. In Tibetan we call it *Rigpa*, a primordial, pure, pristine awareness that is at once intelligent, cognizant, radiant, and always awake...[17]

This clear open space of infinite awareness within is a place where we can always know that we are basically good, basically open and innocent, basically fresh, awake and aware no matter what happens to us. The place of awareness is the place we heal from, come to feel safe in, feel grounded in, and know that our potentials and all things spontaneously arise from this source. The place of our awareness is the healing source within us. It is who we truly are. Being aware in the Now is what many people call coming home. I call it our home base from which we begin anew many, many times a day. Come home to your breath, your belly, your seeing, hearing, just being. Come home to Right Now.

Nyoshul Khenpo Rinpoche, a great Dzogchen Buddhist teacher, said of our Buddha nature, our inner mind:

> Profound and tranquil, free from complexity,
> Uncompounded luminous clarity,
> Beyond the mind of conceptual ideas;
> This is the depth of the mind of the Victorious
> Ones.
> In this there is not a thing to be removed,
> Nor anything that needs to be added.
> It is merely the immaculate
> Looking naturally at itself.[18]

Working with this habitual untamed mind of ours is an endless task until we are ready to discipline it, willing to stop our acting out on others who we think of as responsible for our problems.

A man came to see me recently who had been fired from several jobs because he couldn't contain his anger. He reacted with acting out and insulting comments when criticized or when his feelings were hurt. He said he had to "go with it" when his anger arose. This would often happen at important meetings where there was a lot at stake for him, as he was an art director for an advertising agency.

He was a creative man who valued his talent in his field. He had told himself that he would just have to get away from people who were as narcissistic as he was, which meant all of the people currently at work. He spoke viciously of his particular boss who he thought was a master liar and who had turned on him recently in a meeting and betrayed him as he saw it.

Although Mike had a good understanding of his narcissistic disintegration when someone took away his sense of being recognized, he had never been able to stay present in his anger and pain, let it be, play itself out and shift on its own without acting it out. Much of his thinking was about others whom he called "disturbed" or "crazy." He thought of anger as "the enemy" instead of as energy asking him to pay attention to something it had to say. Mike tried to deal with his pain intellectually by blaming the other person. He wanted to be hypnotized out of this pain. He wanted "the pink bubble" of imagery, he told me, to put his pain into. He told me he didn't want to stay present in it and "wait for it to transform."

He asked if I would give him a Buddhist meditation practice to do when he got angry. I agreed and said it would only work if he practiced it. A first part of this way of healing anger, I told him, was to agree to take good care of himself when he was in the energy of his anger. His anger was energy sensation, I said; that anger told him how hurt he was by something that was happening. Under the defense of anger was the hurt he felt when someone didn't appreciate or validate his abilities. Mike transformed the hurt into anger energy, I said, which was how he could bear to live with the hurt. I said in this exercise he was going to be asked to make a pact with himself to take good care of himself when the feeling of anger arose; otherwise this practice wouldn't work. He would have to acknowledge the beginning of anger arising in himself so he could make the pact to take good care of himself for at least five minutes as he was aware of the anger arising.

I told him I knew he didn't want to have to do this, as it was a piece of hard work, and I knew he would prefer it if someone else could do this work for him, or someone would take care of him when he was in this kind of anger. Until such a person came along, I asked if he was willing to do the work. He said he would. I said he had to agree to take care of himself until someone else came along to do that job, and he laughed.

I said that when he got anger sensation signals from inside his body, he was to close his eyes for a moment. If he could not close his eyes, then he would just acknowledge silently that he was going to take good care of himself for five minutes and be with his feelings, which were energy. He was to breathe in and out of the anger energy, and on the in-breath say in his head, "I am really angry," and on the out-breath, "I am going to be good to myself." He, of course, could pick any phrase or sentence he wanted to say on the in- and on the out-breath, but it had to be something about his anger that was simple and reflected his inner experience with body sensations of anger energy. And he had to agree to be kind to himself during the practice. He was to agree to breathe in and out this way for ten breaths. After that he was to ask himself if he noticed any shift in his body, and if he did, to notice what kind of shift that was, and if not to return to his breathing for another ten breaths saying the mantra another ten times.

I repeated that the most important thing was to agree to take good care of himself in these angry moments and to focus on his breathing, say his mantra, and notice the shift inside his body after the ten breaths. I said that his anger was understandable from the causes and conditions that led up to it. That he acted it out was not okay, as it was costing him his livelihood and his two children couldn't live on air.

The agreement we made was that he was going to observe and stay present in the sensations of anger in his body when they arose. He was going to close his eyes a moment and say to himself, "I'm going to take good care of myself. I'm not going to act out. I am angry and will breathe with it, then it will shift. I will respect my anger but not act it out. I will trust that my anger will shift when I give it a space to exist and honor it without acting it out. I know I'm not my anger. I am awareness."

I asked Mike to use his potential for being present with his anger. His concept that his life shouldn't require mindful effort and discipline was that of a baby. We would all like some mommy there to take our anger away and give us love instead. We would like to be babies and act it out and get our way. But when we act it out and then we don't get stronger or more compassionate inside. When we face pain and stay open in it, treat it with compassion, the pain feels heard and seen, then it shifts. We never know what will come forth as we enter into the experience of the moment, but we do know it will shift and we will end up in a good place inside, for true nature or spirit has only life supporting potentials.

The steps I used with Mike to bring him into his anger and ease his acting out were:

1. *Acknowledge the painful feeling, knowing it is there.*
2. *Acknowledge the causes and conditions that have brought up the anger.*
3. *Create an intention to do the work of staying present, showing up for ourselves, generating openness to what we have.*
4. *Understand that we have to do some work and not act out since acting out would hurt us as a consequence.*
5. *Make an agreement with ourselves that for the next few minutes we are going to take good care of ourselves, be compassionate toward our pain.*

6. *Agree to do this work even though we wish someone else would do it for us.*

7. *Inhale and exhale and stay aware as we begin the work.*

8. *As we breathe, find a mantra to say out loud or silently with each in-breath and out-breath describing the state we are in and our intention to be kind to ourself. For example: "I know I am angry" (in-breath). "I send compassion to my anger" (out-breath).*

9. *Breathe in and out and say our mantra on the in-breath, then the out-breath for at least ten breaths.*

10. *Notice if there is any shift in our body sensations. Notice where we are right now inside, what we are experiencing. The breathing will be repeated another ten times if there is no felt shift inside.*

11. *Continue to stay present with yourself for a few more seconds to validate that you have just done an important piece of work on yourself. You have been willing to not act out and to stay present until your pain energy naturally shifts on its own when you recognize it, and let it be. Notice what you are experiencing right now.*

12. *Know that you are not your feelings, you are awareness.*

13. *Become aware of what is happening inside and outside you now.*

Many such Buddhist mindfulness practices are helpful in dealing with heavy emotional states. When something painful happens to us in our life, the most helpful thing we can imagine is for someone to allow us to tell the truth of what we are going through so that we don't have to lie and suffer the strain of fictitious being. We want to be heard and seen in our truth when we are in pain. We want to be allowed to be, not have somebody come along and try to prop us up or tell us what is wrong with us for feeling as we do. The worst thing is when people try to cheer us up when we are collapsing inside. When we are in pain, we need someone to bear witness to it and stay open with us, stay present without opinion. A therapist really is open and compassionate with themselves otherwise they can't offer that to clients. If they are not open they are just messing with the client's mind.

It is very transformative when people feel that they don't have to go through their pain alone, that someone will stay present with them and available to them and not be afraid to face the intensity of their pain, and not judge them as they are being themselves as their experience unfolds. You are not afraid when you have seen people go through deep pain and seen how they come up in a good inner space for having faced it. *Love is as is. It doesn't ask for anything to be different.* This kind of love that we offer clients and ourselves could be called bearing witness to what is happening. Bearing witness to our pain is healing our pain, as Zen Buddhist teacher Roshi Bernie Glassman points out in his book *Bearing Witness*.[19]

When I was a beginning therapist, I was continually in tension about what I was supposed to be doing which I thought was to fix the pain I saw. I felt the pressure of trying to ease the client's pain or my own. I was not convinced that the truth of their unfolding experience in the moment would set them free. Now twenty years later I am completely convinced.

I saw a woman who was losing her two-year-old son to a fatal neurological disease in which the baby was becoming increasingly paralyzed. During the year, Sara and I prayed together, meditated together, and talked over how this could happen to an innocent child. Her child's suffering didn't make sense to either of us. We spoke of karma, life after death, her sense of being punished for past deeds, her son's mission in life, what she was to learn. She railed against God, and prayed fervently for strength to be with the pain of her rage and sorrow, her feelings of being lost and helpless. What she could do was to be, to grieve, to stay present with her feelings, to breathe into her pain, to see her experience honestly, to respect anything that she felt, sensed, or thought. Nothing she could do would make it okay.

Sara constantly asked me of afterlife in the Buddhist view, passage through the bardo and life eternal. She wanted me to explain to her "beginningless endless" from Buddhism which I did as best I could. She asked me for books and her favorite topic was life Eternal. She and I contemplated these topics. She asked me many times to describe this place called Source. She and I talked over Nisargadatta Maharaj's book I Am That *and I gave her books of Stephen Levine and Sogyal Rinpoche.*

One day Sara missed her chair and fell. She stayed bent over and asked me to hold her the rest of the session, which I did. She slipped out of my arms and lay down on the floor. She asked me not to leave her. There were sounds of agony moving through her. I stayed present, and felt her grief. She asked me to come to the funeral, let her rest afterward in my waiting room and cover her with a blanket.

Her doctor told her the next week that Matthew was going to have to go on a ventilator. At the time all there was for her to do was to open herself to the different experiences she was having. She wasn't "in charge" of what was happening. She "tried" to surrender but it wasn't possible. With Sara, I couldn't pretend to know how to make meaning of her suffering. It seemed the only way was to be together, keep company, bear witness to what was happening. Our work was to value all of her experiences no matter what. Sara said one day, "I work with this moment by moment," and I agreed that this was the only way. As Matthew lay dying, Sara felt rage, for her mother who had not loved her as she loved her son, hatred for her father, and disappointment with her husband who could seldom bear his own pain or hers.

Love and compassion and strength came through Sara as she stayed with Matthew in his final hours. We prayed together for strength and courage and love to face his final hours of precious life. I taught her the Tibetan Buddhist practice of Tonglen[20] of sending and receiving to generate compassion.

I asked Sara what God would say to her if he could speak to her directly, and Sara said, "He would tell me that Matthew taught me how to live and how to love. It's the first time in my life I've let myself be who I am." I gave Sara Buddhist metta meditations of loving kindness for herself and her family.[21] I gave her Stephen Levine's meditations,[22] one of which she used at home. At her child's funeral, Sara read a eulogy and she thanked me for "being present throughout with an open heart. We faced this together soul to soul, heart to heart," she said of our work.

Sara's potential for being present with her own experience and valuing it, her love, her strength had been largely lost to her since she had been a child. It was when her own child was dying that she began to find these again. She began to trust just being herself, with whatever arose. Healing potentials emerged in her to support her when she needed it, when she let herself be as she was. Facing the not-knowing how to be let her live with the variety of her ways. Buddhist wisdom teachings of the four transforming thoughts that redirect the mind,[23] seeing Buddha in all,[24] the Bodhisattva vow,[25] truth and love in everything,[26] Lojong practice,[27] Tonglen,[28] Metta Meditations,[29] were all profoundly helpful to Sara at this time of her life. Nisargadatta Maharaj's views on eternal presence were comforting.

❧   ❧   ❧

Andrew Harvey, a mystical writer and spiritual teacher, writes of the experience when life tears our heart open in a spiritual context in his book *The Way of Passion*. He says:

> "What the master does, in fact, one Sufi Master once told me, is quite simple. In the stage of expansion, the Master takes the heart and opens it endlessly, tears it endlessly open. And when it is totally torn apart, totally ruined, shattered, totally expanded, then the whole universe can be placed in the heart."[30]

As grief burns our ego, our pride, our idea of how life should be, we empty ourselves of who we thought we were. As love lost tears us open, we fall, and falling we find our inner freedom to be the truth of who we are — the loving, beautiful, powerful vital essence that we learned to hide our whole life since our parents couldn't give space to its beauty.

Life tears us open with one event or another such that at some point we have to surrender to the will of God or to that which is bigger than our personality. Only out of the process of being present, in the particulars of our life can the potential for self-value emerge. This potential has often been sleeping in us since childhood. When we are not taught how to value how we are, we live a life that is unreal. We live a lie when we don't value what is happening inside of ourselves as it is. *Love is as is, it doesn't ask for anything to be different.* In seeing this, we have seen the elephant.

A client of mine, named Eleanor, was upset that she was in chronic pain with arthritis. She began to take medication, much against her wish. She had worked with guided imagery with me a few months. She felt that she had created this illness with her anger, grief, and frozen sexual energy. She was

*working with guided imagery at home and considered it
another failure that she still had a lot of physical pain, though
somewhat less. She saw that her vicious attacks on herself were
hurting her, not helping her, keeping her attached to her
mother's view of her as a crazy person because she chose to live
in New York City, to live without alimony, and to do spiritual
work. Ellie still identified herself as her mother's daughter,
and the mother of her children. She had never considered the
spiritual question "Who am I?" in depth. She defined herself
on the basis of how her mother and children saw her, even
though she spoke clearly of the holy spirit within her and felt
its presence.*

*One day we began to locate her anger in her body. I asked
her its weight, shape, depth, texture and to pay subtle
attention to its movement. She went inside her body, cleared a
space, and felt her anger as a hard, solid mass in her chest made
of rock. She saw some "streams" on the upper right part of the
rock, trying to "glow out." I asked her to find the right
distance to observe the rock, close or far enough to feel
comfortable, and to see how "the streams" were moving or
pulsing or what they were doing energetically inside the rock. I
asked her to see the streams in the rock and to pay attention to
them, especially in "the glow."*

*As she kept her eyes closed, she said that these "glints" or
"streams" in the rock were "sort of like streams of love." She
saw the streams as "veins bringing blood, or oxygen…they are
carrying veins. They carry little glints of light to me
sometimes." Ellie started to cry as she began to first listen to
the faint, frail voice of love within her rocklike, rigid attitude
toward her suffering. For the first time in months she was
being respected and open with what she was living inside
herself.*

Following the session of guided imagery with the "love glints," Ellie came in:

E: *I've been in a dark place beating on myself. This isn't helping.*

D: *What are you experiencing right now?*

E: *I feel ... like I would like to put this dark part out of me.*

D: *So imagine doing this now. Take the dark part out and set it aside. Imagine doing that. (Ellie closes her eyes and is quiet.) Can you put that dark rock part outside of you, as if you were putting it on the table?*

E: *Yes.*

D: *Take a few breaths and see what you are aware of now in your chest.*

E: (Closes her eyes.) *My chest is tired and wants to rest. I would like to give myself something.*

D: *What would you like to give yourself?*

E: *I don't know. Something...* (Silence for a few moments.) *I want to look at the gold veins in me, but I'm afraid. I don't think I'm supposed to look. I'm afraid I'm going to be punished if I see this. I'm gonna get it.*

D: *What's going on now inside your chest?*

E: *It's like... I'm not supposed to be somewhere. Something or somewhere where there's sun and I'm not allowed in that room.* (She's in her imagery.) *I can see the sun coming in and I'm going to get it if I stand there.*

D: *Where are you now?*

E: *I don't know. Somewhere...it's funny and she hit me... I don't know where...*

D: *Stay with this...let it unfold on its own...*

E: *I know...I stayed too long. I wasn't supposed to be there, and she's smacking...* (Ellie crosses her arms, across her chest.)

D: *You're remembering being hit somewhere where it's sunny....*

E: *Somewhere at the beach...* (pause) *my aunt's house. I'm in somebody's room, full of sun. I'm on the floor looking out the window...and she came in and started hitting me... More hitting ...* (Pause.) *I don't know why she's doing it...'cause I was in Auntie's room. I'm not supposed to be here. Then we went to the beach, and it was light on the water. I never saw it before. And I think... I'm thinking...* (Silence.) *I'm not supposed to go there. I went in there. I didn't tell her...* (Silence.)

D: *What's going on now, Ellie?*

E: *I sit there and she hits me, across the face, and hits me and smacks me* (making gestures). *I'm scared to leave the room. I'm scared she would push me out the window.*

D: *Uh-huh.*

E: *Hit and hit.* (Ellie is angry and she's moving her arms. Her voice is strong.) *I would like to beat the shit out of her for coming in without my permission.* (Ellie laughs spontaneously and continues for a few moments.) *No wonder I like to go to the beach and take all the time I want.* (Ellie begins to shake her head back and forth.)

D: *What are you experiencing?*

E: *I feel very strong. I feel strong. I want to hit* her *for telling me what to do. I don't want people to tell me what to do. Don't tell me what to do.* (She says loudly.) *All the fuckers that tell me...all the time* (screams). *Don't tell me what to do.* (Opens her eyes and looks directly at me.)

D: *You don't want the fuckers to tell you what to do.*

E: *My mother tells me I make myself sick. She says I do it...as if she fucking knows. How does she know why I'm sick? I'm also not sick, but this she* doesn't *know* (laughs)... *Art tells me what to do with my kids, and Janey never calls me. When I get her she tells me she has five minutes to talk. And fucker Doctor S. tells me that I know about stress and where it comes from...meaning my head. I'm mad at God for never making me pretty after the nose job. There isn't a person who would cry more than two minutes if I died right now.* (Ellie begins to cry and laugh intermixed. Then there are a few moments of silence.)

D: *You think people would cry two minutes if you die....*

E: *This hurts me. Really hurts. Really, really...gets to me...*

D: *What?*

E: *Maybe they care. I think they do, but...it makes me sad...this I really can't hear* (Ellie opens her eyes and looks at me. She closes them again.) *Yeah...there is something...so* (pause)...*I feel so much how I feel, just feel now...so amazing...like little lights coming in me...for how I care...and it isn't only me...and my mother might care...* (Silent. Ellie appears deep in her own processing.) *It's like the little streams of light make a passage to something I want.*

D: *You want something?*

E: *I don't know...I can't say.*

D: *You can't say.*

E: *No...I just can't say...make a passageway to something I really want. I know, but I can't say.*

D: *Yes. Something's coming up in you, you want...*

E: (Shaking her head very slowly and then being quiet for several moments, then opening her eyes.) *I don't know what to say. There are no words. It's surprising. Maybe I can ...be loving even with the hard rock in me.* (Silence.) *I want to say thank you, even though...I just want to say that.*

D: *Right. I hear you.*

E: *Well, I'll see what comes from this....*

D: *You have love inside you.*

E: *It just came up...but I can't say it...the word.*

D: *Yes.*

E: *I'm afraid...really afraid...I feel us being here and even though I want it...to be here, I'm really afraid.*

D: *Yes. There's a lot here now in you and with us.*

E: *Yes.... It's funny to have love and see I have it and see I'm afraid to have it.*

D: *Yes.*

E: *You're the only one who gets it about me.*

D: *And you? You get it.*

E: *Yeah, I do.*

Ellie has closed off her need for love because she didn't believe she would get it. She wasn't aware that the universe had another agenda for her. She identified with the object relation of rejection and on the level of content grasped at it by going over obsessive monologues in her discursive thinking on how she deserved to be punished and was a bad person. She held on to this structure with her mother by rejecting herself. She tried to believe that she was in control so that she could second-guess her own tenderness. Yet on an intuitive level she did have faith, for she did come to psychotherapy and she did continue to inquire into her inner life with courage and strength.

Sharon Salzberg speaks in her book *Loving Kindness* of metta, which she calls the revolutionary art of happiness.

> The practice of metta uncovering the force of
> love that can uproot fear, anger, and guilt,

begins with befriending ourselves. The foundation of metta practice is to know how to be our own friend. According to the Buddha, "you can search throughout the entire universe for someone who is more deserving of your love and affection than you are yourself, and that person is not to be found anywhere." You yourself, as much as anybody in the entire universe, deserve your love and affection.[31]

Throughout everything, our potential for love remains intact, pure, and available to us when we find a person who gives us the space to be as we are, and hears and sees whatever way that is.

Sharon Salzberg goes on to say:

We so often in our lives serve as mirrors for one another. We look to others to find out if we ourselves are lovable, we look to others to find out if we are capable of feeling; we look to others for a reflection of our innate radiance. What a tremendous gift to enable someone's return to the awareness of their own loveliness.[32]

Ellie is still afraid to leave her mother and live her own "loveliness" where she could enjoy sitting in the sun and looking out the window. She is afraid to grow up and enjoy her life. Instead she clings to her mother's view of her, and keeps herself company with her mother's voice in her head. Ellie is in a constant court battle with her mother in her mind, always winning or losing her case. Her mother taught her that it was wrong to be at the window, delighting in the warmth of the sun and looking at the light and space everywhere. How simple and pure life is when our superego and object relations don't get in the way.

એ   એ   એ

Our felt experiences in our body seem frightening because they don't fit in with our conditioned beliefs of what should be happening in our life, which is just another story. There has been a major culturally developed habit that says the physical body is nothing more than a slave of the mind. When our mind considers what is going on in the body dangerous, it asks its slave, which is our musculature, to contract, to make a shell, to stop something from happening that we perceive as different from what we were taught to believe is okay. Then we continue to live in our shell of mental constructs and attach ourselves to it as if they were real. On the level of content, things are judged by how they look, what others think, the image they cast in a world of illusions. We focus on the shell and try hard to perfect it.

The mind has been trained not to trust feelings in the body, and to doubt that it can work with the bodily sensations and feelings and energy since they were too terrifying to bear alone in childhood. The thinking mind uses its own logic and interpretations to shut down the regions of the throat, the heart, the solar plexus, the pelvis, the stomach, the genitals, or all of the above. The mind shuts down on giving and receiving energy in the body's emotion centers, or chakras. Although we may talk in therapy about what we are afraid of, and some movement can be made at solving our issues intellectually, no real change can be integrated or maintained until the physical shutdown or contraction is recognized in the body and our experience is directly felt in the body.

We don't argue with our breathing or close it down. If we tried to close down our breathing there would be a life-threatening situation, and yet we are always doing this with our feelings when we contract and move into our head and try to jump-cut to solutions.

In a process of compassion for ourselves, in a process where we are valuing ourselves, are merciful to ourselves, we begin to become aware that what is necessary when pain occurs is not a kind of shutdown, and not a superego attack or judgment, not an opinion of wrongness, but rather the understanding that we need highly sensitive and delicate care for ourselves, compassionate care for ourselves when we hurt. All of our feelings and thoughts just want us to be there. Our body and mind are just asking for our compassion and the clarity of awareness. We have two friends who need our comfort. They are called: Body and Mind.

The body, mind, and spirit in us are equipped with a caretaker, which is awareness. When awareness is brought to our pain and we stay present we are giving ourselves care, and healing ourselves. When conscious awareness is withdrawn from our sensations in our body, we are no longer giving care but are involved with thinking about pain, fabricating stories about pain, making interpretations that it is good or bad. To be aware of our pain when it happens, to let it be until it dissolves is taking the very best care of ourselves. We can treat pain as the beloved.

The pain that we all feel as part of being human can never be healed by turning our back on it. By making mental activity out of pain, we are dulling ourselves. Some of the pain we experience is about an injury occurring in our energy field—because we won't let energy come into and move through the body. We then feel hungry, isolated, lonely, dead, depressed, and so on. It is we who are not allowing in what the other person is giving us as energy. This close-down is our fear of being Present and receiving the energy and love we must have to nurture our life. The fear of staying present is there for good reasons, but there is a time to be willing to see what the truth is in the present as it arises.

J. J. Krishnamurti often used to say "The word is not the thing."[33] We believe that our labels, our definitions, our concepts, and opinions *about* it are the same thing as *what it is,* and they're not. *Now* is the only place life goes on with a real flow of energy. Suffering occurs in the distance between what is fact, and what we make up.

Joel Goldsmith in his book *The Infinite Way,* speaking of wisdom, says:

> The cool clear water of the well of contentment within refreshes you with the assurance that joy already IS. "Peace be still."[34]

Why would we want to work with someone who has the view, who believes, as Freud did, that in psychological work we will find "common human misery" within? Spiritual practice introduces us to what Rumi says, which is more reflective of our true human nature. We don't have to keep chasing elephants in the tangled jungle:

> The small ruby everyone wants
> had fallen
> out on the road
> Some think it is east of us, others west of us
> Some say among primitive rocks, others
> in the deep waters.
> Kabir's instinct told him it was inside and what
> it was worth,
> and he wrapped it up carefully in his heart
> cloth.[35]

ও   ও   ও

Psychotherapy has not understood the spontaneous power of our true human nature or the wisdom within for healing. As spiritual work continues to come into focus in our culture, we can see how we are always forming and unfolding from the open space of awareness within. A Buddhist teaching called Great Prajna Paramita Heart Sutra has taught, "Form is emptiness. Emptiness is form."[36] Forming never stops when we empty ourselves of concepts, when we stop clinging to our interpretations and judgments. Our potentials are confined only by our clinging to conditioned thoughts.

I talk with clients of awareness and simply being as where our inner healing potentials are in seed form. For them to flower we have to stay present. We all want to heal into our connection with one another. In the next few years psychological work will focus more on the importance of awareness and being, resilience and positive resources, potentials and healing, process and flow. I recently heard the story of a friend who went to a famous analyst who took notes all during the session. She felt unconnected and asked him if he could be with her and she told him his writing bothered her. He looked up from his notebook and said, at age seventy-something, "This is the way I work. What do you feel about this?" My friend looked at this old man so trapped in his intellect, and said, "My heart is breaking for you," which he wrote down in his book.

I read this at a workshop I gave for therapists, counselors, and healers recently:

> How is healing to be found?
> How is fullness to be found?
> How is peace to be found?
>
> When you enter the moment as it is arising
> When you are one with it.
> You are empty of "me"
> Being nothing, you are everything.
> Here it is found.[37]

Roshi Robert Kennedy has an anonymous poem in his book
Zen Spirit Christian Spirit:

> The way not to drown
> Is to
> Swim far out
> And dive deep down.[38]

And that is where the elephant lives!

Endnotes

1. Nisargadatta Maharaj. *Pointers from Nisargadatta Maharaj,*
    by Ramesh Balsekar (Durham. NC: The Acorn Press, 1982),
    p. 169.

2. A poem from the author's guided imagery class, New York
    City, 1995.

3. Alia Johnson, a statement from a Diamond Heart class,
    New York City, 1996.

4. Note found on a scrap of paper with the author's
    handwriting.

5. Diane Shainberg class on integrating spirit into
    psychotherapy practice.

6. Tulku Urgyen Rinpoche, *Rainbow Painting* (Boudhanath,
    Hong Kong: Rangjung Yeshe Publications, 1995), p. 57.

7. Deepak Chopra, *The Seven Spiritual Laws of Success* (San
    Rafael, CA: Amber-Allen Publishing, 1994), p. 9.

8. Namkhai Norbu, *Dzogchen: The Self-Perfected State*
    (London: Arkana, 1989), p. 4.

9. *A Course in Miracles* (Foundation for Inner Peace, 1985) pp. 1.

10. Eugene Gendlin, *Focusing*, (New York: Bantam Books, 1982), p. 14.

11. Tao Te Ching, translated by Gia-Fu Feng and Jane English (New York: Vintage Books, 1989), p. 27.

12. J. J. Krishnamurti, *The Wholeness of Life* (San Francisco, CA: Harper & Row, 1979), p. 156.

13. Longchempa, "Cloud Banks of Nector," Crystal Cave, trans. from Tibetan by Erik Pema Junsang (Kathmandu, Hong Kong: Rangjung Yeshe, 1990), p. 106.

14. Pema Chödrön, *Start Where You Are* (Boston, MA, and London: Shambhala, 1994), p. 33.

15. Pema Chödrön, *Start Where You Are*, op. cit., p. 34.

16. Roshi John Daido Loori, *The Still Point* (New York: Dharma Communications, 1996), p. 51.

17. Sogyal Rinpoche, *The Tibetan Book of Living and Dying*, op. cit., pp. 46-47.

18. Nyoshul Khenpo Rinpoche, *Natural Great Perfection* (Ithaca, NY: Snow Lion Publications, 1995), p. 96.

19. Roshi Bernie Glassman, *Bearing Witness* (New York: Crown Publishers, 1998).

20. Sogyal Rinpoche, *The Tibetan Book of Living and Dying*, op. cit., p. 193.

21. Lama Surya Das, *Awakening the Buddha Within* (New York: Broadway Books, 1997), p. 126.

22. Stephen Levine, *Healing Into Life and Death* (New York: Anchor Books, Doubleday, 1987).

23. Lama Surya Das, *Awakening the Buddha Within*, op. cit., p. 126.

24. Lama Surya Das, op. cit., p. 136.

25. Lama Surya Das, op. cit., p. 142.

26. Lama Surya Das, op. cit., p. 152.

27. Lama Surya Das, op. cit., p. 151.

28. Lama Surya Das, op. cit., p. 161.

29. Sharon Salzberg, *Loving Kindness: The Revolutionary Art of Happiness* (Boston, MA: Shambhala, 1995), pp. 29-32, 97.

30. Andrew Harvey, *The Way of Passion* (Berkeley, CA: Frog Ltd., 1994), p. 84.

31. Sharon Salzberg, op. cit., p. 25.

32. Sharon Salzberg, op. cit., p. 26.

33. J. J. Krishnamurti, *Talks of Krishnamurti in Europe* (London: The Krishnamurti Foundation, 1969), p. 97.

34. Joel Goldsmith, *The Invisible Way* (Marina del Ray, CA: DeVorss Publications, 1947), p. 153.

35. Robert Bly, *The Kabir Book* (Boston: Beacon Press, 1977), p. 44.

36. "The Heart of the Perfection of Great Wisdom Sutra" (New York: Zen Center of New York Service Book, 1985), p. 2.

37. Notes from a seminar given by the author at Mani Center for Integral Psychotherapy, New York City, 1998.

38. Anonymous poet, Roshi Robert Kennedy's book, *Zen Spirit, Christian Spirit* (New York: Continuum Publishing Co., 1996), p. 76.

5

Experiential Process

How joyful to look upon the awakened
And to keep company with the wise.

Follow then the shining ones,
The wise, the awakened, the loving.
For they know how to work and forbear.

Follow them
As the moon follows the path
Of the stars.[1]

Eido Roshi, who is the teacher of the New York Zen Study Society, met with my husband and me about teaching a group of therapists how to sit zazen meditation. We spoke to him of the interest of friends of ours in learning to meditate and he was willing to come and teach us. For me sitting was a mecca from my everyday whirlwind with two children, a house to run, clients, and so on. We invited twenty people in the late 1970s to come over. Everyone arrived hushed, tiptoeing around. Eido Roshi was clear, answering many questions including the standard "How can we be making a difference if we are just sitting here?" or "I can't go back to my breath when I am fascinated with my thoughts. How do I make myself do this?" etc. What was impressive was the way he responded to all the questions equally. We took our stuff—zabutons and zafus, blankets and shawls, Kleenex and amulets, to sit down and face the wall. Eido Roshi came to teach us three times.

After eight weeks of once-a-week sitting there were four people left in the group. Most people told us that they were too busy, other things had come up. One woman had spoken of her "terror" in the silence. A friend said that she couldn't stand the sound of swooshing through her ears. After four months there were three of us left. Of the three, my husband became a student with J. J. Krishnamurti, I became a Buddhist priest, and my friend later moved to Kansas City to spend time studying Zen Buddhism with a teacher there. Most of the therapists disappeared into the pressing affairs of everyday life. Each spoke of their gladness that they had "tried." For several years I sat alone resonating with the invitation of silence to let myself be.

Lex Hixon, a spiritual teacher, quoted a poem from the third koan of Keizan Zenji's Denkoroku in a book written just before he died, called *Living Buddha Zen*:

> Continuous stream plunges
> over ten-thousand-foot palisade.
> No dust mote comes to rest
> On this pure silk
> that forms our seamless robe,
> this awareness always dancing
> and singing, "Buddha is alive!
> Buddha is alive."[2]

It is this dancing alive awareness of nowness that is always waiting to come forth. We just have to loosen our grasping onto conditioned thoughts.

It is said in spiritual work that the form of one's faith is seen in the form of one's readiness for life. Faith is readiness. Each of us lives our own private, self-created structure of faith and faithlessness.

In his book on his awakening process, *Do You See What I See? A Message from a Mystic,* Jae Jah Noh says of his journey to awakening and of faith:

> Even though one may not be prepared to face some form of truth, still, if he is willing, he is ready. Readiness has nothing to do with preparedness. One is never prepared, there is no preparation for life. If you are here, you are prepared.
>
> How do you know when you are ready? You are ready when you are willing to be ready. *Your entire existence has been preparation for the moment you are now living.*[3]

In Buddhism we learn that each of us is a jewel reflecting every other jewel in the net of Indra which is cast over the universe. It's a whole fabric in which each of us is a piece. When somebody's got soul you can see it in their eyes and body. They have gone deeply into their heart. They have gone deeply into the specifics of what they are experiencing.

In Dzogchen practice they see the sky as a metaphor for the awareness that is everywhere — open spacious and vast. We are given meditation and spiritual practices to discover our innate natural state, our Presence, our Being. So in this state why close out anything? Left in our natural state we are content, and all of us are born with the inherent freedom of being. It's not something that we have to construct or fabricate. We don't have to obtain it from elsewhere. It's called our True Nature, our Buddha nature. By nature we're all Buddhas. Our only task is to awaken to what we truly are below the layers of defenses and mind structures.

Waves are not separate from the ocean. Our conflicting emotions are part of us. They don't put us in bondage. It's identifying with them that puts us in bondage. Grasping onto them puts us in bondage. Left as they are, our emotions simply arise and pass. When we give them a space to exist, they dissolve. The waves are the content of our mind. The water out of which they're made is awareness.

We have lost remembering our center inside, and we feel lost, fearful, and confused on the earth. It isn't that we don't know what we are here for, but we don't know the miracle of existing. We have learned to cut off our connection to our inner experiencing. I often think of Liz, a woman I saw in my office for several years when I see the dazzling-looking women on the New York City streets. They walk so nobly, dress so elegantly, laugh so easily. What is going on inside of them? I saw Liz as one of these apparently "together" people.

As a child she had twirled around on the beach until she fell over to find her sense of connection. Then a bit later in her life she rubbed her hands and feet until they bled to find it. She dug her hands in the earth in the California forest to feel something real, and later she clung to any man she could find to give her a sense of existing. She had sailed around the world to connect with the elements, but she couldn't be still long enough to face her many experiences inside, letting herself just be in her natural process resting in her senses and her own thoughts and feelings. This location of experience inside herself took her a year with me to find.

I want to give excerpts from a couple of sessions with Liz to convey that it is a major struggle for those locked out of their inner world in childhood to enter it again. Fortunately we have support from our innate potentials to make this journey. It is facilitated when the guide recognizes and validates these emerging potentials as they arise and lets their process naturally unfold.

Liz is gifted, blessed, and tortured. She was forty-six when she came in. The first time I saw her she told me of twirling on the beach as a child in union with the sky and stars, her way of feeling connected in a family where she was abandoned by her mother and father. Her mother lived in a narcissistic shell of getting more, and her stepfather didn't want her. Liz was a mystic who wore the daily mask of a tough political city planner. She was beautiful in appearance and dressed as if she had come off the pages of Vogue. She was brilliant, alive, laughing, moving, talking, gesturing in a way that was funny, driven, tense, and engaging. We had an instant connection. Liz was a woman lost to her own feelings, brilliant at pleasing others, not knowing who she was from inside.

Liz came in hearing that I practiced spiritual work. She had a background in Christian mysticism — feeling connected with forest divas and God since she was eight years old. She came to me because she had physical symptoms of burning in her body. She had seen doctors, neurologists, astrologers, and psychics about this. I was part of a list of people to whom she articulated her burning sensations. The burning occurred at certain times when she was on overload, which was often. It occurred when she was afraid that her commitment to the bureaucracy of the city couldn't go on since it was "lies," her relationship with a married man couldn't go on since she felt she was made for him but he disappeared from her life for stretches of months. She was involved with a man who gave her money in exchange for occasional sex. He was thirty years her senior. Liz was in pain with burning in her limbs and on one side of her body for part of each day.

Liz told me of several men she was sleeping with. She talked of how she had "fucked them all," and gotten large city contracts for her firm this way. This was interspersed with taking Percocet during sessions "so the pain won't split my head open."

She told me of a time in her twenties of having spent a year on a sailboat going around the world with a group of men for whom she was the cook. She hooked up with them at a marina and decided to do it on the spur of the moment, as she loved space and light. She knew none of the men and loved the whole year of moving around, settling nowhere. For a while in her late teens during high school, she had lived in some woods in California "among the trees" communing with God, always rubbing her hands in the earth between the trees, digging in the earth to try to "ground herself." I said I felt she might have been trying to locate herself inside, looking for her own Presence or looking for a way to be herself and find comfort. The agony of Liz were her losses and that her very Being wasn't welcomed, seen and appreciated by anyone.

Liz spoke so fast I couldn't understand her some of the time. She had a crazy, wild sense of humor, making fun of shrinks, crazy people, maniacs, "sex-crazed people like herself," New Yorkers, mystics, Jesus freaks, rabbis, her church group, the world of politics, builders, artists. All of this swirl would then suddenly stop in each session as she would merge into my eyes with a gaze of fear and ask, "What do you think is really wrong with me?" She would then be intensely quiet as if her life depended on what I would say. The mersion was intense. I felt she was absorbing my being. I spoke of her having been locked out of her feelings since childhood and spoke of possible aspects of burning from this. One aspect of "burning" could be a longing to live inside herself, which she was distracted from doing. We spoke of so many metaphors of burning, including "God's blaze" in her that brought her to an urgency to express her brilliance and passion for life in her relationships and work.

I felt sometimes with Liz that she wanted transmission of what life is. I spoke to her not of what was wrong but of what was – right now – with her experience. "Where are you right now in your direct experience? Let's give a few minutes to see what you are experiencing in your body." Each time I would speak of her experience in her body she would tell me that she didn't think that she could go on with her life. She was in terrible fear – that her life was a lie, that the man she loved would never divorce, and she would be screwed out of work by someone younger and prettier. Without a penis in her, or soon to be in her, she felt empty and deficient. She said burning might be her need to "release into something, surrender into something which I cannot do." I said her readiness to surrender to the truth of the moment from inside was important.

Liz spoke of feeling "horny" and "driven." She spoke of men, jobs, money, and survival. She was in some pain physically from burning at times and went to a new neurologist. Many diagnoses had been ruled out, then she would go back to check it out again – although she seemed convinced that what she had was "stress induced." This kind of instant disconnection to what she actually was in contact with from inside her body was apparent, and I spoke of inquiring into the stress in her body, which I asked her to describe in some detail. She couldn't focus on it.

She was always on time and showed me her new clothes, shoes, drawings, books, told me her thoughts and dreams. She came twice weekly.

I had faith in her unwinding into contacting her inner experiences as I listened. I did not try to change her tempo, but I did want to move her more into some awareness of her inner experience. I validated and mirrored her interests, her yearning for orgasms, creative longing, experiences of lying, fear about survival, coldness with her mother, spinning, burning, fear.

Liz soon told me that she often took certain painkillers on prescription — just "in case I feel pain. I usually feel pain during the day, the burning." We spoke of burning out karma, burning away the ego, burning the sickening shell, burning up with the longing to have Mark be hers, burning up mad as a child when her father left suddenly when she was five years old and her mother took her to her grandparents and left her there to go off with her boyfriend for three years, burning in feeling at one with God, body burning sending her a message when she is overtired, the burning with passion to live every moment of life, still burning up in fury with her mother who didn't know her and couldn't be present and in contact. I remembered A. H. Almaas' writing of the "burning" that neurologically comes when you can't rest in the arms of your mother because of "negative mersion."[4] We spoke of this. We spoke of burning until you can surrender in a moment to where you truly are inside and then let yourself relax and rest and Be. I encouraged her to practice this opening into her experience in my presence and let herself Be wherever she was.

Some of Liz's flight was to get away from a kind of pain she had experienced intensely at five and six when she was alone at night in her grandparents' house on the cot she slept on in the dining room. Liz had been "parked there" for three years while her mother was "having an affair." Her father had left when she was five and no one was sure where he had gone. She found him twenty years later. Liz remembered lying on the cot and having a "burning," feeling agitated and lonely. She would sometimes go into her grandparents' bedroom and stand there until her grandfather would take her into the living room and hold her. Sometimes she would rub her hands and feet until they bled to stop the "burning and itching" inside her. She had a doll she would talk to, and sometimes she would get up and walk around and twirl around until she fell on the floor and would then crawl back into bed exhausted. It was clear that Liz would do anything not to feel her anguish and fear, which was too painful for her as a child to bear alone. It was too painful for her to feel her losses in childhood. Her frenzied movements kept her from feeling the agony she was in. She was tying to protect the precious part of herself which she had keep hidden since she was quite young. She couldn't be herself for fear of her loss. Liz connected her burning as a child to "feeling completely alone."

We began to speak of her loneliness and where it was in her body. I asked her for its location in her body, its size and shape, texture, depth. I asked her to stay and allow herself to notice its movements. This session is the first time after a year of therapy that she could locate anything in her body as experience from inside, stay present and be with it as an ongoing felt experience.

I asked her to go into her body where the pain took place, which was often on the right side. I asked her to be with her experience of this pain as she noticed it in her body, and to be aware of the sensations in it, the energy in it. I asked her to stay aware and notice what was in there in the right side. Liz closed her eyes. She said that she was starting to feel warm and not burning, and that she wanted to open her eyes and just breathe with me. She did this. I asked her what she was experiencing now:

L: *Me and you… I want something. I need something… I'm afraid you'll throw me out or get sick of me 'cause I want so much.*

D: *Is that what you are feeling in your body?*

L: *Not now.*

D: *What are you directly experiencing in your body…in your chest or pelvis, in the front part of your body?*

L: *I sort of... I feel with you, but then as soon as I do, I think you'll be fed up.*

D: *You feel with me in your body?*

L: *I'm more relaxed, but I know this won't last, and that the pain will come back. It isn't here now, not at this moment.*

D: *Let's see what you experience...just notice...in your belly or your chest.*

L: *As long as I'm with you or someone I don't feel so much. I have some burning when I don't have anything to do, or somebody to be with.*

D: *What can you locate in your body right now in the front?*

L: *Right now I can worry that you will not like me, but I'm not worried about that right now.*

D: *You're without worries at the moment?*

L: *(Laughing.) I don't want to worry... I worry I have, like, MS or cancer, but I've had all that checked. I worry a lot that I'm making myself sick with burning both ends of the candle...like I always have to go, and run, and having someone's dick in me. I'm not really living.*

D: *"Not really living" — can you allow a space to get a felt sense of "not really living?"*

L: *I don't think my work is meaningful, not even creative. I don't stay with a man; when I fall in love the man disappears, then I'm worried that I won't ever find Mr. Right. This pain keeps me sort of company — like my doll, so I don't have to know too much.*

D: *The pain keeps you company. What is it that you already know?*

L: *That I'm pretty alone. There's some way I can't get what I need from someone else, and not from myself either.*

D: *What is it you need from yourself?*

L: *I guess not to feel lonely and afraid...and afraid that I will be lonely again, and more of the same.*

D: *The thoughts about being alone bring on the pain.*

L: Yes. I want to know how to deal with this pain. *What do I do with it? I think someone can get me out of it, and they do, but then they go away, and it comes again. I want someone to stay with me forever and never go away.*

D: *You want someone forever. You have this pain with people leaving you. When you open your body into this pain, what do you experience?*

L: *I go to bed... I can stay in bed, or just cuddle up with myself. I do that and I feel like I can rest in my blanket, but I have to have a lot of pain.*

D: *It sounds like you can respond to your pain sometimes, with caring. You don't like this pain, but sometimes it opens you to some kindness for yourself. You go to bed, you cuddle up with your blanket. You know it's in your body. You can take care of the pain in your body at times. You can witness it with compassion.*

L: *I wouldn't have the pain if they didn't leave me or I wasn't so afraid of their leaving....*

D: *Your thoughts focus on someone leaving. This is interesting how you heal your bodily pain sometimes. When you listen to it and respect it and really give it space to be, then you finally rest in bed. What happens when you can do that...go to bed and snuggle up with yourself, be kind to you?*

L: *I'm exhausted. And I know it, and when I finally do lay in bed, sometimes I cry... I don't even know why. Tears just melt out of me, like my chest is just melting...like now...*

D: *You have a feeling inside your chest...a melting.*

L: *I am surprised I can do this 'cause I was taught to hate my pain, to tough it out, to twirl around until I drop. But when I'm too tired to be afraid...then I don't have to keep moving.*

D: *Tell me what you experience now with this melting sensation.*

L: *I can be with it, kind of like my grandfather...just sort of tuck myself in, snuggle, melting into it.*

D: *Yes. Opening and melting into your body...*

L: *Grandfather love...*

D: *Grandfather love...*

L: *What a word. I can't even believe I used that word. I was a hyperactive kid... I am* (crying suddenly)... *I don't believe how that word... Well...I really* (a few moments). *I can't believe how much I want to cry to think that I could even think that I could be loving. Well, you never know what's going to happen.* (Liz smiles and shakes her head.)

D: *You can melt into that loving feeling...inside.*

L: (Quiet) *It's hard to believe... Yes. I guess so. Although I don't think of myself as loving. I never thought I could. But I guess I can...*

D: *Find love inside.*

L: (Laughing.) *Yes...*

As a five-year-old, Liz couldn't face the hurt of losing both her father and mother. Her father had disappeared and her mother had given her to her grandparents for several years. Her grandparents didn't want her at the time. She began to lose her contact with herself and began spinning into activity, twirling, running from experience, afraid to be with herself and what was happening inside.

Liz learned to survive by pleasing others. She found her potential for love right in the middle of her pain when she finally faced her pain and went to bed where she could melt into what she was experiencing. Then loving feelings for herself emerged. She is burning physically, partly out of the wound of getting separated from the possibility of being herself as a child, the truth of her own experience, the truth of her own loving feelings being unwelcomed. Liz recreates the experience of not being loved by her mother in her symptom of burning. She is now afraid that there is no real love for her anywhere. She runs from her experiences out of fear of being hurt again. In this way, she has kept herself from feeling her pain, but also her frenzied activity has kept her from her inner potentials for healing. She discovered some lost aspects of herself in this session. Her compassion, love, courage, clarity, intelligence, self-value, and honesty were all right there to support her when she stayed present and was aware of what was happening inside her in going to bed.

How does one receive? One has to be still...and listen...and turn toward oneself.

"What do I do with my pain?" Liz asks me at some point. Here are some ways to reflect on this:

> *Experiencing our pain is the cure for it, for when we experience it, it shifts and something new begins.*

> *Awareness of pain is the cure for it. Sending an open awareness into the bodily sensations of pain eases it instead of fighting it.*

Being present with our pain is healing, for as you let it exist, it liberates itself and the new moment arises with new potentials and experiences.

There is only peace when you leave things as they are.

If you look the whole world over you won't find anyone more deserving of your love than you are.

You have the heart of a lion, in truth. Pain is worth going through to find your own truth.

When you know that love is continuous as awareness you won't be so afraid of pain.

Make room in your heart for your own pain. Nothing is permanent when you leave it as it is. Let it be as it is, and it shifts.

See the pain within you as wanting to be noticed. Open up to it and listen to what it says. It wants to be noticed. When you notice it, it feels heard, and eases, then dissolves.

We don't believe that love is enough, but it is enough to burn away our attachment to our old beliefs.

Allow your heart to be aware of its own truth whether there is pain in there or not.

Feel pain in your body as energy. See how it is moving within. Stay present in it. Follow the inner movement. Watch it shift.

In the process of awareness, our pains inside dissolve. Where there is awareness there is healing. Stay open and aware in your bodily sensations and your pain will self-liberate.

Touch with kindness and awareness what you have formerly touched with fear and your pain will shift.

An open heart is a much greater gift than illness is a tragedy.

Start giving yourself kindness. The process of healing is stumbling and falling and getting up, and starting all over. Start fresh right now.

When we are being in the truth of the moment we are in alignment with the highest potentials. They will then unfold inside of us to support us if we stay present.

Be sure not to lock yourself out of your own heart.

You can't change anything until you acknowledge what is there, and how it is — then change can happen.

Without judgment, be with it. Meet this set of sensations with your heart, not your story about it.

All of us are in pain. That's the human condition. But we can send compassion into it, and see that we're not alone in it. Then it will pass on.

It sounds too good to be true that what we have to do to change our life is to stay present and recognize our experience in the moment, and stay open and respectful until it transforms. Yet it is so.

Healing our pain is learning to open to the truth in the moment, as we saw with Liz. For Liz this was a surrender in her bed of being in too much pain to go on pretending.

❧ ❧ ❧

After this session the burning sensation Liz came into therapy with eased, and seldom appeared for a while. In her second year of seeing me she fell in love with a woman. This woman was a teacher in the Church. Liz was madly in love, yet said she wasn't sure she was a lesbian.

Our work was to find ways to encourage Liz to stay present and in contact with her inner experience so that she felt stronger and more clear. Now after one year Liz was looking for the positive mersion experiences she had missed with her mother. Conflicts for her came out in moving into closeness and beginning to individuate and differentiate. This was a painful and joyful set of experiences — her discovery of being able to be herself with another person.

Liz described Sandra as "powerful and strong as a mountain." She said when staring into Sandra's eyes she felt she disappeared in a good, melting, merging, way. She had never felt this warming, opening of her heart before in her life. I saw Liz as recreating mersion experiences, which were probably mostly negative with her mother. As she did this she internalized some greater sense of groundedness and contact with immediacy. These early life experiences of being unwanted, unloved by a busy mother, left at five with a grandmother who didn't want her, left her neurophysiology in tension, burning, wired. She was not able to come to rest inside. With Sandra she could just Be.

Liz began the session I mention here with a vivid description of the "ecstasy" of the co-creation of a writing project with Sandra. They left Sandra's apartment in early evening and walked together to the subway stop. They stood on the street staring into each other's eyes. Liz said it was an experience of "eternity." She said they simply couldn't tear themselves apart. She said she had an intense need for this gazing, merging: "It is so intense it feels close to madness. Then later I feel scared." I asked what the madness was exactly, and she said that they both became still when they did this. They didn't move or want to move. She felt she couldn't be anywhere except gazing deep into Sandra's eyes. She said being in such intense, open contact frightened her afterward. She said:

L: *I'm paralyzed from this. It makes me nauseated. I have a terrible pain in my throat.*

D: *What sort of pain? See what's in there.*

L: *I feel tight, like I have to choke or speak, but I can't.*

D: *You can't find your voice?*

L: *Now, yes. But with Sandra I feel there is this mountain. There is a mass I can't get beyond. I can't move it. I begin to feel sick...and angry. There is a force there. I don't know what it is.*

D: *What's in this experience of a force? Unpack it, see what's there.*

L: *Yes. I remember this woman from* Woman in the Dunes, *the movie. When I saw that movie I was alone. It made me so sick I couldn't walk out of the theater to go home.*

D: *What made you sick?*

L: *This woman was imprisoned by her mind. To be trapped in the prison of your mind... I can't bear it.*

D: *What's trapping you now in your mind?*

L: *I stand there with her, and I feel trapped. I can't move forward or leave. She stands there too we stare at each other for long times... It scares me. I was staring at her and I couldn't leave, I started feeling angry.*

D: *What is in it that brings anger or fear?*

L: *My mouth feels sick. It may be I don't want to be a lesbian. I'm not, but then I want her to take over my body and do with it what she wants. I want her to take me over...but I'm afraid...really afraid.*

D: *What is in this energy of fear? Stay with the sensation of fear. Just be aware of what comes up.*

L: *It's like having dinner with my mother two nights ago. We never connect. My mother has no idea who I am. She's telling me how she has this crush on her doctor, and how she wants to have an affair with him. She starts telling me the horrors of living with Jake [Liz's stepfather] and how he was never able to give. Then I ask her how come she married him and my mother says, "I had a child. I had to marry. This ruined my plans!!" And my mother is talking to me like a stranger. I want to say, "I am that child. Why are you talking to me like I don't exist? Why don't you see that I am that child who you are always saying ruined your life?" I want to say, "Who do you think you are talking to?" But I don't. She has no idea she's talking to me, that there is a person in me...that she is affecting me.*

D: *Your mother doesn't see there's a person there...that you exist in a wonderful way of being you.*

L: *She doesn't even know I'm there. She's talking to herself.*

D: *Does this bring nausea?*

L: *It makes me gag. I can't talk. My mother won't see. She's busy with her affairs. Sandra is strong, though...and grounded. She makes me talk...she won't chitchat. I'm gagged with her too.*

D: *What gags you?*

L: *I feel my mother is nowhere. I can't find anything inside of her. But Sandra wants to own me...she wants to overpower me and own me. I know it...she would never see it this way.*

D: *Your experience is that Sandra wants to own you. You sense this?*

L: *I feel it. And I want this, but also I want to be free... I want to jump inside her body...go in through her vagina and I'm afraid it will be very dark inside of her and sort of dangerous or grim. Then when I'm inside of her I want to have my spirit float out her back and sort of unfurl outside where I can see the sky... I want all of this...to pass inside her and then be free... I want to see the sky and dance and open my arms and laugh and see men... I want to be with Sandra and then be playful with men and have my freedom.*

D: *You want to be merged and then be free, enter Sandra and come out when you are ready. I guess you want to feel you can come out into the world when you are ready and practice being yourself...then go back inside. Maybe you get frightened when you're not given the freedom to be yourself. She wants to trap you in there, you feel. With her you feel she will leave you if you do what you want. You need her to let you come and go in your unique way.*

L: *No one ever let me go because no one ever knew I was there. Sandra knows I'm there. She sees me. She loves me. But she won't let me be free to do what I have to do. I want to come and go. I want the closeness and then to go out in the world and be free.*

D: *I hear this. You want closeness and then freedom.*

L: *(Quiet.) I do. But I want to leave also. I can't stay all the time.*

D: *What will happen if you stay all the time?*

L: *Then I get angry. I feel Sandra's anger. She wants to overpower me. It's her show. Everybody at the church loves her.*

D: *When you stay present and stay with Sandra, you are feeling her anger, and you feel you have to hold it like you always hold your mother's anger and pretend it isn't happening. You can't talk about it...your mouth and throat get stuck instead. You have to pretend that Sandra is the saint and your mother is a wonderful mother who made sacrifices for her daughter. The lies are beginning to nauseate you maybe.*

L: *I feel that I want to enter Sandra but not go deep inside her body...deep in is a darkness and depression.... It feels like I enter the dunes of imprisonment if I stay. My mind starts working when we move into creative work. I want to go in, and then go through. I want to fly free, but I can't move. That's because I feel her angst... I can't just be with her. I can only for a while, then she wants to own me and she's mad at me. She won't let me be the way I am. Then I feel angry or afraid. And she is angry.*

D: *I hear you want to be where you can be and be loved for being yourself. What are you experiencing right now?*

L: *I'm afraid I can't be myself. I'm mad that she overpowers me. I'm afraid she'll leave me.*

D: *It's like you are five years old again, and you want to go out and play but then come home and feel safe and loving with some stable mommy who's always there for you. You want to explore the world and have Sandra be there to love you. She is opening up love in you which you have been longing for, but you're angry at the demands she is making. This feels like rapprochement, wanting to go out and then come back home to be loved and be your precious, unique Being.*

L: *I feel how much I love her...and she spoils it with her demands. I get angry that she thinks she can call the shots 'cause she has the power. I want to go through her into the sky and be free. I want my chest to be open... I want to be me. And find somebody to love me.*

D: *Yes... I hear that.*

L: *She freezes this...'cause she wants me to commit. I can't be myself then. I'm angry. Why won't she let me be me?*

D: *Being present in your experience you see you are holding many feelings...the wanting to stay and be who you are, and the wanting to have freedom too. This place of being present with Sandra is different than the chitchat with your mother and brings up feelings of longing to be close and yet free to be yourself.*

L: *It feels like too much for me. I have to flee or get paralyzed.*

D: *You are being present in your experience, you can welcome your experience and notice where it goes. You create a space for witnessing it, and not having to think whatever you're feeling is, good or bad. What are you aware of right now coming up?*

L: *I know she won't let me be me. I know it. With Sandra, now I get angry and then the thought that I can't exist without her.*

D: *Who are you taking yourself to be when you think you can't exist without her? Aren't you the four-year-old who couldn't stand it when your mother left? It's an old story. It's not the truth anymore. You can be aware of your fear and not think its your totality. You can witness your fear with compassion.*

L: *I need her to survive. I can't live alone. I can't go back on this. It's too late.*

D: *Who are you that you can't exist alone? Alone doesn't go on forever. Can you exist one moment at a time?*

L: *Now I want to be with myself...just be.*

D: *Yes.*

L: *I'm very sad...with everything. It's so hard...to find myself and keep it and not give it up. I don't think Sandra will keep me. No one will.*

D: *What are you experiencing now?*

L: *I feel like my chest is breaking,... I'm almost fifty years old and...where will it go? I'm afraid. What am I supposed to do about Paul or Sandra?... I'm breaking apart. I thought I could have it all without pain...just relate like my mother did with no struggle. I honestly don't know how to be myself and be with anybody else. I don't know what to do. I want her, but I can't give up who I am.*

D: *What is in your chest? Stay with your body a moment. Let the sensation be in your chest.*

L: *I guess it's softer in there… I don't know.*

D: *You feel softening in there.*

L: *Doing what I want.*

D: *Uh-huh..*

L: *Staying with my experience. You mean…*

D: *And honoring what's there.* (Silence.)

L: *I'm afraid…* (Silence.)*… I won't be anybody.*

D: *Just being…*

L: *I could, but nobody will let me.*

D: *Let yourself be…and let it all unfold naturally.*

L: (Breathing more deeply.) *I feel really heard and I feel… I can just stay here…and I don't have to figure it out. What if Sandra leaves me? What if Sandra stays with me? You know, I try to do the thing that will bring me the most. I'm a real schemer. I want her, and I want Paul. My head won't stop. What happens if I want to be free? What if I have to be all alone? What if I make the wrong move?* (Breathes) *I want to stop all this…and I can't.*

D: *Just being as you are. Just this moment…*

L: (Begins to breathe softly and closes her eyes, then curls up in the chair and is silent for a few minutes.)
         I feel I have to trust my feelings or I'll be killed. Let me stay here and rest… I need to rest.

D: *Yes.*

L: *I see what I do to myself. I try to please everyone. Then I get terrified and have to fly away. It's hard for me. I'm afraid you want something from me. Afraid you'll leave me. Afraid. Afraid. Afraid. Oh, my God, I won't let myself be.*

D: (Silence for a few moments.) *What's your experience?*

L: (Silent.) *I feel good... I can let you be here a little.* (Liz breathes more deeply and closes her eyes and rests curled up.)

We sit for some minutes as Liz breathes quietly and rests. *We rest in just being together.*

In this process Liz is struggling to be herself and value her own experience. Her feeling is that she wants to be with Sandra and then wants to have her freedom to be and do as she wishes and return when she wishes. Liz begins to realize how frightening it is for her to stay present in relating. Liz begins to experience the fear of someone else not giving her the space *to be* herself which we practice in this session and many sessions to come.

As there is space for Liz to be wherever she is in session, she calms down and comes to rest. Liz clears a space within to see that she can't go on like this trying to please everyone she meets, giving up her inner power, and remaining mute. Out of this session comes a potential for presence that Liz has never felt before. We spend many subsequent sessions with Liz "practicing" being with herself and her direct experience, discovering how calming and strengthening this is to find her home base of awareness inside from which she can hear her thoughts and feelings. She learns not to abandon herself.

As Liz begins to live more out of her inner experience, she begins to tell Sandra some of her experience without the terrible fear of abandonment, for she is no longer leaving herself so much. She begins to own some of her own value and power in her relationship without having to project these potentials onto Sandra.

Staying present in our experiential process is at the heart of spontaneous healing. It is the work that brings awakeness and awareness and the present moment into our life so that we can see and feel who we actually are. We can find inside the elephant we have been chasing if we choose to turn to ourself.

We always raise the question of trust in experiential process work. There are deep places within where we can trust a basic goodness, a softness within, where we can center ourselves and know there will always be awareness and our breath and our Being as a home base to start anew. We can always return to Right Now for a fresh start.

A client began spontaneously thinking, "Nobody wants me...nobody wants me...." The thought arose from she knew not where other than the flow of life deep within her at that moment. Feelings of sadness came up. A terrible fear of being without support came to her. She felt no one ever wants her if she is vulnerable. She felt isolated and alone. Images of floating in the air as a baby, wrapped in a blanket and alone, appeared clear and vivid. The client cried for several moments, and said, "I see a light or lamp. It's in the room. There are no people anywhere. I'm lost and alone." "Stay present and be with your experience," I said. She began to rock. She simply sat for long moments in her old wound of having no one she could contact in her family as a loving presence. She rocked in her chair, and said, "I have the light in the window. I know it's there. I have my blanket. There was no one, but I had the light in the window. I knew I came from that light."

For the past fifteen years, I've done a silent retreat each year in the Zen or Dzogchen Buddhist tradition. Each time I enter the meditation hall for a week or a few weeks of silence, I know that most people in the hall will cry in sorrow or in joy during our time there. Most of us will break up laughing at some point at the cosmic joke of who we've taken ourselves to be. As we sit, we see the way we have identified with the structures of our mind, with our conditioned scripts. As we meditate, our images and identities open out from egoic self-concepts into boundaryless awareness that extends our view of who we are. As we open into the moment, we see how vast and open we always intrinsically are. All the clouds can pass without upsetting our spacious openness.

ॐ ॐ ॐ

A woman recently told me, "I didn't come to see you to see how unhappy my marriage is. I came to fix it, to make it better." This woman wants to fix it without experiencing the way it is. Wanting something to be different without knowing *what it is* is the ultimate confusion—unless you recognize it, it won't transform. I spoke with her of inquiring into her actual experience of being with her husband. She said there was a "brute fear" in her that he would leave her any minute. Then she said, "I don't want this fear."

I spoke of fear sometimes arising as a protection and sometimes out of a sense of not being able to live the truth of who we are with another person. We become afraid as we feel ourselves selling our soul for the approval from someone else. I mentioned that often fear, when it arises, is asking us to care kindly for it, let it tell us its story. Like anything that's here, it wants to be recognized and treated with respect. When we hear it, it softens and dissolves and shifts.

I encouraged the client to understand that her main work on herself was to know when she was afraid and not to hate it, and to let it be until it revealed its message. "When you notice something with respect, it eases and shifts," I told her. *"Feeling is a wisdom bearer.* Listen to what it has to say. To try to lie and hide from fear makes fear an outcast, and it more desperately bangs on our door. When we answer the call and listen to it, it relaxes and speaks and dissolves.

"Now let's inquire into your relationship to your fear." She said, "I hate it. What am I supposed to do with my pain?" This is one of the statements I hear most often in therapy, as if pain were not supposed to happen in life, or if it does, it is something we have to get rid of instantly. This way of seeing comes out of our lack of understanding that when we recognize our pain it naturally shifts and something new arises. It was her reaction to it and contraction around the story about it that kept it locked in place. "Trust your pain, it tells you where you are. Begin to bring awareness to your pain, for it is there and wants to be acknowledged. Then it will go away. You will then be stronger inside for facing it. *The more you know of who you are, the more you are.* Stay with it and see what is inside of it. Where in your body do you sense it?" I spoke with her of how her hating her fear was what made it worse. I asked her how she learned to hate her fear instead of to have compassion for it. Her ideas of life said pain is a bad thing and she is a bad person to have it. Pain brings shame, she told me. Pain is a set of sensations in the body, I countered.

Carl Rogers said in *Becoming a Person*, "When I accept myself as I am, then I change."[5]

I said to this woman, "Step back a few feet from your pain, give it the distance you need in order to witness it. See its color, or size, its way of moving, when you look at it, its shape. Witness it, stay present, and see if it shifts. Witness the energy, the pulsations, the tiny movement, the rhythm that's there in it. All you have to do is recognize it, and it will feel heard. Stay back the distance that you need to observe.

If you sit on a mountaintop and watch the sun and the wind begins to blow, you might say, "I lost the sun." But it is there glowing in the grass next to you. The sun is everywhere; you can't lose it. The spiritual is everywhere. We tend to think we can only find it in the light. But that is like feeling we must stay on the top of the mountain to experience the sun. Find its reflection everywhere, even in the darkest places and then you can't lose it.

Right in the middle of the fear is a space for the courage. Right in the middle of the symptom is the prayer.

Process work brings people to life. Experiential process work involves these steps, which are the process of healing into being ourselves:

1. *Turn inward and be aware of what is arising in you.*

2. *Recognize it, see it, hear it, sense it, feel it.*

3. *Let it be, leave it as is.*

4. *Stay present and open in inner experience to notice what is happening in sensing, feeling, thinking... and let it unfold on its own.*

5. *Know that you can act clearly on the basis of what becomes clear to you from what you see and sense in the moment.*

6. *Return to your six senses (five senses plus thought and feeling), and see what is going on inside of you right now.*

7. *Show up and stay present and remain open. Be aware of the flow of life.*

8. *Leave things as they are and appreciate that they can only be the way they are at this moment.*

It isn't that we haven't developed our potentials; it's that we haven't been still and at ease and present with ourselves long enough to give them an open space in which to arise. We have been too involved in our mental self-preoccupied activity to be present and recognize what's happening. We don't need information in order to change. We need wakeful presence, human contact, and finding the truth of where we are, in order for flow to start again and inner transformation to begin. Psychotherapy has often deluded us into looking to our habitual mental activity for healing. Can the conditioned dualistic mind heal itself if it doesn't tap into experiential unfolding awareness moving through us moment to moment?

Most of us were not encouraged to share what we were aware of as children. No one may have listened to what we were going through. So we tend to look at ourselves from the perspective of the outside, of our identity, and not the reality of what is arising and unfolding inside of us that got forgotten. As we are open to our experience, we discover the love of being ourself, which we still have no matter what our history. What hurts us so much is how we were separated from our contact with our Being — our unique way of being.

Our inner truth never causes suffering. Lies do.

It is the pull of habit and ego to resist our aliveness and spontaneity and passion, which we were taught to resist as kids. Our lively presence was too much for our parents. Ego doesn't know who we truly are and has no interest in our finding our highest potentials, our intrinsic Buddha nature. Ego works to keep the structures of the mind intact. Ego doesn't know that we are much more than mom's and dad's scripts and that we can hold the whole universe in our awareness. Ego doesn't know we truly are awareness and not our thoughts and feelings.

We learned to be afraid of our strengths and passions, joy and spirituality, our vital essence as children. Our mental structures keep us believing we are babies incapable of making choices in our life in this very moment, and believing we are not It, and this is not It. Our ego clings to the idea that we cannot trust the universe. Our conditioned beliefs say, "What difference does it make? I'll never get what I want." Our spirit says "Wake up and live. It's a magnificent dance!" Thinking mind says you are your ego. Spirit says you can live wisely by paying attention in Right Now.

I have never seen anyone who stays present not be delighted and humbled by their spontaneous inner process where the fountain of life pours forth in plentitude.

What is our training as therapists for this openness, this wealth within, this resiliency, this not-knowing, when we don't cling to the discursive programmed mental activity? In our psychological training programs, we don't practice this.

In a state of awareness we do not take ourself to be the object of our mind but rather the subject of our heart. An open heart is a greater gift than illness is a tragedy when we are awake. The great Indian spiritual teacher H. W. L. Poonja who taught so many current American spiritual teachers said in his book *Wake Up and Roar*:

Student: Who is graced with grace?

Poonja: *Everybody.*

Student: Why do so few people hear it?

Poonja: Those few know that they have it. Others don't. For thirty-five million years you have been doing. When you finally reach a true teacher, he will not ask you to do anything. He will say, "My dear son, come and sit quietly; Be quiet. That's all. Don't do anything... Go to the heart right now. No time to waste. Heart is very near. How far is the heart from you? Mind you, there duality does not exist... This is the teacher and this is the teaching. Stay as your heart, that's all. (Laughs) Stay as your heart.[6]

No matter how much we kick and scream about our life, we have to start where we are. We have to start here and deal with those aspects and qualities that are in us and in our life right now. Each one of us is a perfect representation of exactly where we are now. We can't be any other way. Why don't we see that we are graced by virtue of being on this Earth. We are graced with existence and presence which are the miracles we have been given.

Jane walks into the consultation forty minutes late. She speaks hastily about the subways. She tells me with hostility that I am "on a list" of therapists she is interviewing. She said she might not be able to "let me know today if she wants me or not." She then asks me, "Who am I?" because she has seen a few "people" and she can't remember what "somebody" told her about me. I mention some sentences on who I am. Then she tells me I look upset. She says she doesn't know if she can go on in this "quest" for a therapist as her life is falling apart and her husband won't impregnate her as he thinks she is too hostile to have his baby. At this point we have no time. I suggest she come again and say it is frustrating to have so little time to talk. She says it must be amusing to me "to kick people out of my office." I ask her to come again and talk, as the buzzer rings for someone coming in.

"Next," she says, enraged. I explain to her how to exit from the building and which door to close.

Is this person making sure to be "thrown out" as her pattern? Maybe. However, the fact is, Jane showed up. Her rage is externalized, but this rage, in itself, is where she is. Seen with respect and given a place to exist it will easily shift to hurt for being denied her wish to have a baby. This anger contains her enormous energy for her transformation. It will lead her into her own heart if she stays present with it. Why won't she let herself be seen and heard for longer than ten minutes right now? Perhaps the pain is more than she can bear or the shame, the rage, the frustration. We see her potential for strength, and for being present in the ten minutes she was with me. She stayed present with her anger and humiliation. I mentioned my wish to see her again. She came again months later. This is where we started — furious, closed out, kicked out, humiliated, judged, misunderstood, rushed, hostile, acting out. With Jane I was frustrated too. Yet we made contact in the midst of it. This potential for contact was coming through despite the mess, and my sense is that we both heard it.

Here are some important things to reflect upon, which I say to clients to encourage them to stay present in their process work. *Processwork is the basis for psychological healing.*

- ➤ *When you stay open, the things you lost inside arise. Give what is arising a space to exist, stay present and you will begin to see arising the potentials you lost in your childhood.*

- ➤ *When you stay present there will be a shift inside of you.*

➢ *Allow what is coming up to unfold and open a door into your heart. See what other doors open, what you go through.*

➢ *It is by going through the pain or wound that we get to what is ever-healed, the source of all life, our true nature, our spirit, pure open awareness.*

➢ *Trust your heart to see and know what process you need to go through right now. Trust the universe to support you in your healing by sending you what you need to heal.*

➢ *We have to go through the pain to get to the strength, love, vitality, and other potentials that flow out of our true nature deep inside. Our potentials for healing will flow forth if we stay present.*

➢ *Pay attention to what your body wants to say, your senses tell you. Stay present with what is happening. Respect and honor it.*
Let it be.
Watch it change spontaneously on its own, and simply witness everything openly.
See with clarity what there is to do next in your life.

➢ *When you enter the moment as it is arising, you are complete, and full; you are content. Whatever could be lacking in a moment when you are fully in it?*

➢ *Be with life within and you can be satisfied. It will always change. "Know thyself." Enter within and replace the lies with being yourself.*

➢ *Learn to trust your inner process. It is your inner teacher. Inner process lets you discover what you have inside. You have to get out of your own way to let it flow. Then arrive in the moment. Let yourself be a finder not just a seeker.*

➤ *Bring the inner sensations, feelings or thoughts into awareness, and hold them in awareness, and watch them change. Know that by practicing being aware you make more room inside for life without being upset by it.*

➤ *Let go of holding on to your thoughts.*

➤ *Be quiet. Lay aside your story and stay with your energy. Surrender into what is happening. Be quiet and present, let things be, receive the new moment openly.*

➤ *Feelings are collections of inner sensations of energy. They are asking to be recognized, acknowledged, and heard by you. When your parents didn't listen, you were in pain. You are still in pain when you don't listen. Be there for yourself in the way you want others to be there for you.*

➤ *When you are in your experience in an open way, you see that whatever arises will self-liberate or pass. This means that everything changes, nothing stays the same, nothing stands still. This means that everything is workable. Everything is correctable on its own. When you let things be, true human nature will replace your habitual ego patterns.*

➤ *Gradually let yourself be aware of what you carry around with you. See clearly the bodily sensations inside your pain, what hurts you. See what your body is holding as sensation. It wants to be seen and heard, validated, and honored like anything that is right here. Let yourself recognize what you experience, and see how it shifts.*

➤ *When you leave things as they are "it" will take care of itself according to the laws of nature, just like a flower bud knows how to open or a leaf to fall.*

➢ *Let your feelings be anything they need to be. Don't judge what arises in you. Don't believe it isn't enough or it is too much. Everything that arises is equal with everything else. Mother Nature is brilliant and sees everything as equal yet unique.*

➢ *Move the process from your head into your heart, into your body, into the area of your chest, of your heart. Surrender into the moment, and stay in your heart. You will notice a shift in your feelings or thoughts. Recognize the shift.*

➢ *Everything in consciousness is moving. Let the intelligence and energy that you are keep moving as it naturally will. Let your inexhaustible wealth from within begin to unfreeze and move through you in its natural way.*

➢ *Don't get in your way with your head and self-attacks. Stay open.*

➢ *See the difference between the bodily sensations and the story.*

➢ *Be with yourself and see what inside of you is asking for acceptance.*

➢ *Know that you are not your feelings and thoughts. You are the awareness that can witness them and doesn't have to identify with them. They'll dissolve when you are there for them.*

➢ *See what is being revealed to you. Let it expand and tell its story. "It" will pass when it is ready.*

➢ *Truth and love arise from the same place healing happens – in open awareness.*

➢ *Be with your heartfelt feelings, and from the place in your heart, you will know what is right for you to do at this moment.*

➢ *Stay in the place of truth inside your own experience.*

➢ *Come out of your story. Lay it aside for now and come right into the present moment. Let yourself be in the now.*

➢ *See your awareness of your breath, your energy, your sensations, as home. Come home many times a day.*

➢ *You can always choose freedom. Come into the now and see and hear what's going on. Start all over again.*

➢ *Love is as is. It doesn't ask for anything to be different. Notice yourself as is.*

➢ *When judgments begin, tell your judging superego it is not helping, and it is hurting your natural spontaneous healing flow that wants to happen now. The superego is a voice from the past. It has no idea that you're going for a higher truth than it can know.*

➢ *Create an openness and spaciousness to finding out where you are right now. Open to not knowing, and bearing witness. Then you will know how to act.*

➢ *Discover "Don't-know mind." Let "it" tell you what needs to happen. Let "it" move on its own.*

➢ *Our hearts grow strong at the broken places. A break allows us to heal.*

➢ *When we come to recognize the truth of our sorrows by facing them, an unspeakable relief is born in our heart toward ourself. This is compassion for what we have been through and why we had to do things the way we did.*

➤ *Respect and honor whatever arises. The truth will set you free to be awake to the next moment.*

➤ *Get out of the construction business,[7] step back from all the stories of the mind. Disidentify with your self-image and be in the immediacy of the present moment as it is.*

➤ *Disidentify for the moment with your:*
   Identities
   self-images
   self-concepts
   shell
   persona
   beliefs
   superego attacks
   stories
   object relations from the past
   ideas of how life should be

➤ *All these structures are from the past. Be in the immediacy in the present and see what wants to come forth to support your transformation to be as you truly are.*

➤ *"Leave it as it is... rest your weary mind."[8] Be in being, as is. Let yourself heal.*

➤ *Who you truly are is what is happening inside/outside right now. That's why it helps to stay present.*

➤ *Let it happen on its own so your wisdom can reveal itself. Our wisdom wants to reveal itself.*

➤ *Know that in the end, what you are seeking is the seeker. You are seeking to discover your precious being as it is — the preciousness of who you are, in your own process, your own experience.*

> ➤ *Be in your continuum of awareness. This is the key to transforming your life. This is your process for the rest of your life. Be awake to it. This natural flow is the key to healing for it holds all of our potentials.*

In spiritual process work clients heal the separation from themselves. As they allow their wounds and experiences to open, they open a door into their heart. This door in their heart opens to all of their potentials. As they stay with the process, the potentials they lost will arise. This is a major way to heal suffering. In childhood they separated from their own experience of love and that is their greatest wound. There is never a healing of that wound until the willingness to stay present is recovered.

It is experiential process work that shows us how to value and appreciate ourself such that our loving heart is rediscovered. When recognized, our true nature, our pure open awareness sends us everything we need to heal. Our pure awareness is the elephant we have been searching for in the tangled jungles. It is our purity, out of it flows our wisdom. It is our home within. In this home we can be ourselves. Inside and aware we are safe and sound.

Endnotes

1.   Dhammapada: The Sayings of the Buddha, rendered by Thomas Byrom (Boston, MA, & London: Shambhala, 1993), pp. 55, 56.

2.   Lex Hixon, *Living Buddha Zen* (Burdett, NY: Larson Publications, 1995), p. 49.

3. Jae Jah Noh, *Do You See What I See? A Message from a Mystic* (Quest Books), p. 61.

4. A. H. Almaas, *The Pearl Beyond Price* (Berkeley, CA: Diamond Books, 1988), p. 255.

5. Carl Rogers, *I Am, Then I Change* (Boston, MA: Houghton Mifflin Co., 1961), p. 17.

6. H. W. L. Poonja, *Wake Up and Roar* (Kula Maui, HI: Pacific Center Press, 1993), vol. 2, pp. 26-28.

7. Lama Surya Das, lecture, Dzogchen retreat, Canandaigua, New York, summer 1997.

8. Lama Surya Das, lecture, Dzogchen retreat, Canandaigua, New York, summer 1997.

The Beginning of Wisdom

A woman came to see me for several years. She had just been divorced when she started. Her husband had moved out suddenly, her world collapsed. Her mother had died two years before her husband left her. She wanted more than anything to be married and have a family. She had a highly responsible job in investment banking and didn't like her work, boss, or co-workers. She had spent time with her mother two years earlier when she was dying of cancer, flying to where her mother lived in the South several weekends a month. She eventually reconciled her mother and father, who had been divorced many years, so that her father gave her mother a place to stay in his guest house and provided nurses.

Laura and her mother had an intense relationship such that Laura often felt she kept her mother alive with her love and support. She adored her mother, an architect and airline pilot who was seductive and beautiful, had a drinking problem, and had made several attempts at suicide while Laura was growing up. Most recently, prior to having cancer, her mother had smoked and drunk to excess, had walked out into the ocean to drown and was rescued by a stranger. Laura was aware that her mother wanted to die, and Laura's understanding was that after her divorce her mother felt she had nothing to live for. Laura was afraid this was going to happen to her. Laura often cried in discussing her love for her husband and her miserable loneliness after their divorce. Her husband refused to speak with her after their divorce, moved to California, remarried and had a child.

Every step of being on her own was agony for Laura. She was thirty-nine and not clear what she wanted to do with her life. She had been anorexic and was hospitalized as an adolescent. Now she worked out every day, had a trainer, and taught aerobics once weekly in addition to her full-time job. She tried to produce a couple of videos on aerobics and dreamed of being a film maker. Her relationship with her father was stormy. Each time he didn't recognize her feelings or was indifferent, Laura would withdraw in rage, not see him for months. She also withdrew periodically in hurt from her best friend. Laura found a sense of contentment and curiosity in American Indian spiritual work. She became involved with the leader of the group, followed him to the West, and finally had to leave him because of what she felt was a financial exploitation and betrayal over money and unkept promises.

In the course of our work I had used breath work with Laura for a number of sessions, which brought an increasing sense of strength with an acknowledgment and valuing for her feelings of loneliness. After every session, Laura was quieter and more open. She wasn't sure she could go on without her husband, but her spiritual work interested her. I used guided imagery with Laura at times, which she found useful.

During her years with me Laura began to work with a psychic healer who cleared her chakras and took negative entities out of her auric field. She saw a soul-retrieval shaman who helped her clarify her soul's journey and life mission. She worked regularly with her healer, who did bodywork and chakra work with her. She took an aerobics class four times weekly. Her daily job in banking was busy and hectic as she was an executive in the investment department. She was in perpetual motion, going skiing as often as she could afford it. She told me that she could no longer put her trust in any one person, that no part of her "recovery" was better than any other. I said I understood this, and respected her knowing what helped her in her healing process. I felt that this constant running was necessary for Laura not to make too much contact with the pain inside her. I felt she knew when she would be more ready to stay more present and slow her pace.

Laura was angry with her mother for wanting to die, and often remembered how her mother couldn't speak to her with appreciation for helping her the last year of her life. Laura brought me disappointment after disappointment, despair, loneliness, anger, frustration, all interspersed with great laughter we shared about nutty and funny things she observed in the world. Laura's imagery work helped her find the correctives to her early life wounds, and helped her feel the depth of her longing for love. She found safe places inside, and began her American Indian spiritual work after finding an inner guide who was an Indian man in our guided imagery work.

In our work, I validated Laura's healing work, her clarity, her curiosity, her courage, her staying present, her sincere interest in truth, her compassion for her own suffering and her emerging self-valuing and trusting in her own process. I encouraged her to stay present in her experiences of rage, hurt, emptiness, despair, and told her that as she stayed with them they would transform and new potentials for healing would arise.

Laura was deeply afraid of intimacy with men. She had been married for seven years and was always afraid her husband would leave her for another woman, which he eventually did. Her father had done the same thing. Laura often asked me how she was going to overcome her fear of men, and I said many things to her:

> "As you move into your experience of fear
> with openness and less judgment, stay with it,
> and let it be, recognize it and honor it. It will
> naturally transmute into some new energy.

As you open to your fear more, you'll see how it transforms, and you'll contact your courage for going on even when you have it."

"Using present awareness as your home base, as Mother Earth within, you'll be more in contact with yourself and then more open and in contact with others."

"Your awareness holds your fear and is not stained or obscured by it. See that you are the unstained awareness that holds it. Fear will come and go. Awareness of it is clear and open. It is your power to be whole no matter what happens."

Laura said this consoled her. We agreed that it was her choice to practice awareness or get wrapped up in the story about fear which scared her more than the bodily sensations of fear.

Laura began this session by telling me that her mother was with her all weekend in presence and in her head. She said, "I feel she's watching me, and she doesn't want me to leave her. She wants me to keep her company. I hear her telling me, "`You can't have anybody. You can't find anybody.'" Laura began to cry and said, "It's too hard, I can't go on with it."

D: *I hear that. You're hearing your mother's voice in your mind saying you can't have anybody. It's a very rejecting voice.*

L: *She wants me to keep her company.*

D: *And what do you want?*

L: *I'm tired of the whole struggle, because I know that she wanted me to be there with her when my father left, be there after she tried to kill herself, be there when she was drinking and be there when she was dying. She didn't want me to leave her the way her father did... I hate that she didn't want me to be happy. She still doesn't.*

D: Your mother doesn't want you to leave her still. You're still holding on to her in your mind.

L: She wants me to be as unhappy as she was...to be in suicidal despair. Every time I find somebody she says, "He's not good enough for you." I hate her.

D: I see that.

L: I was down to seventy-six pounds when I went in the hospital. I was there five days and they fed me IV. She picked me up...my dad didn't come...of course he was working, but she picked me up and we drove home in total silence. She didn't say one word about what I'd been through...no hugs...and then I went in the house and I knew she was glad I almost died...like she did...she and I couldn't do it...we couldn't find anybody to love us...we were the unlovables...and I felt that her whole life...her father, her husband, her boyfriend...none of them loved her. This weekend I wanted to kill her. I imagined not even seeing her when she had cancer...not going down until she died and letting her know how I knew she wanted to die. I killed her this weekend in my imagination. She asked for me, and I said, "Where were you when I needed you...when I wandered around the house alone... You were busy or depressed or making up for Daddy or buying new clothes for Daddy? When were you with me?" I want her to die in my mind...

D: You feel ready to kill your clinging to her in your mind.

L: I hate her completely... She fucked my marriage. I went there to care for her. She's the one who split us up. She wanted that... (Silence; begins to cry quietly.) It's sad, how much she kept me back, how she hated my excitement and my creativity... (Silence.)

D: What?

L: I just saw this image...me in our house in Long Island. I remember that fear. I was in the house alone and looking for her... She was somewhere in the house, probably sleeping. It was getting dark, and she was sleeping... I was alone, and afraid.

(Laura begins to sob.) *I'm so beat up…so torn up… I'm rotting from lack of love.*

D: *You feel connection with the unprotected child in you?*

L: *Some… I feel her fear.*

D: *You feel some fear of how your mother went to sleep on her…left her alone, wasn't present. What else came up in you for the little girl?*

L: *I feel some tenderness for her…*

D: *Some tenderness…too…*

L: *And you know we lived close enough to the ocean so you could hear it…the sound of it…*

D: *And inside you hold this sound…?*

L: *Well, I'm still here… I go on… I went down every week… No one else did. I have my own sound.*

D: *Yes… your own sound.*

L: *In the sweat lodge I stayed. Some people left or moved, but I stayed. I prayed. I have the sound of snow inside me…ocean and fire and snow… I have my own sound besides weeping.*

D: *What is that?*

L: *Well, to my mother it's "Drop dead."*

D: *Yes, there's that. Any other sound?*

L: *(Quiet.) I always hear the ocean sound. It reminds me that I can stay alive…and somehow find my own life. When I ski, I hear the sound of the snow…I love that sound. I love snow and ocean. Also I love the sound of fire crackling. I especially love the sound of water moving… Once I heard someone say, "Life moves on. Either you join it or you get left behind." My mother is dead…and life's moving. I'm pissed and sad. I feel for the little girl. (Silence.)*

D: Yes...

L: *I feel close to her. She needs somebody to hold her... I feel love for her.*

D: *Yes. You want...to hold her...and a sound of loving her.*

L: *I heard that the Zen people say when you hear the sounds of the Universe you can be intimate with everything.*

D: *I've heard that.*

L: *I want to love. I want to admit that. And I don't want to be alone. I don't want to feel I can't have anything. I want to speak to my mother and tell her she's dead...her time is over. And let her know I miss her, but it's my time to live...*

D: *You're speaking to her now...*

L: *I want to pray to her to free me.*

D: *A silent prayer, or out loud?*

L: *Silent.* (We sit in silence a few minutes. Laura has her eyes cast down. She looks up.) *I have to free myself from her.*

D: *Yes and you are.*

L: *It's a long road. I'm not as afraid as the girl... I walk around afraid but not all the time. I'm glad I could say I wanted to kill my mother. I'm trying to free up the mental hold she has on me.*

D: *I agree. This is such an important process for you, to free up the hold and find more space for your loving presence.*

L: *It's funny. When I think of the sound of the ocean, I think of eternity...and where is my mother... I don't know. I give her a special place in my mind in the upper right corner where she can be safe. But I don't want her to dictate to me. And when I think of snowflakes I remember how they evaporate so easily... They come and go...people, and snowflakes... I really know you are with me. It means a lot even though I can't say it much.* (Laura stands up, opens her arms to me and we hug a few moments before the session is over.)

Laura's process of feeling moves from fear into anger, into sorrow, into memories, attachment to her mother, loss, loneliness, creativity and into some compassion for herself. Her presence emerges when she lets herself be in silence. It is when Laura is being—herself with no agenda. In this session, she sees how she is stuck in grasping ideas of what she can have in her life. She sees her own anger, strength, and clarity in her struggle to free herself from her mother.

We seldom sit down to be quiet and let ourselves be to see where we are. "Let things be for a moment. Let go of holding on to your thoughts." "Go to your heart, stay present, and see what opens" is the best advice to give sometimes. Laura was courageous enough to do this.

In the midst of despair, letting herself be, Laura remembered the silence of snowflakes, the sound of the ocean. *Silence brings us the presence we need as our place of ease within...silence and peace bring growth.* Here is a poem I found in a notebook. I don't know who wrote it.

> Understanding is the
> Ultimate seduction of the mind
> Go to the truth
> Beyond the Mind
> Love is the bridge.
> Stillness the Sound
> Light is the way.

Laura began to remember the sounds of her life. In this being quiet, being as we are, we heal into our intrinsic wholeness, we then live in the dynamism of the totality...with each event that happens. All the sounds of the universe are within us. Be still and know yourself deeply as you are. Laura remembered this spontaneously.

No one in our childhood may have been interested or curious or able to bear witness to what was actually happening in us, so we learned to distract ourself from it, disconnect from it. We abandoned our own truth to receive whatever love was available. The conditions for getting approval and love was often at a high price. It meant giving up our way of being our unique Being.

Every day I hear people tell me they were in the hospital, seventy pounds, almost dead. And no one hugged them, or talked about it. What is going on? Where are we? Every day, all day, I hear the violence we do to each other, how we isolate ourselves, how we hurt each other so badly we can't speak anymore. And under all the protection we know there is a Buddha full of love, this is what kills us — that we can't express the love we know we have.

In this healing process with Laura there are no comparisons with anyone else, and everything arising is spontaneous. As a Zen teacher of mine, Roshi Bernie Tetsugan Glassman said, "Do not try to put your head on top of anyone else's head."[1] When you try to compare what you are with anyone else, you suffer.

It is not helpful to focus only on what is wrong. According to Buddhist perspective, there are problems but they are temporary and they always cover over one's basic goodness. To see problems in the broader context of health is to let go of clinging to one's neurosis and to step beyond obsession and identification with them. The focus in spiritual work is not only on the problems but rather on the ground of experience, on the awareness itself—on boundless awareness out of which problems arise.

This boundless awareness is within. The ground of our experience, our awareness, sees each thing distinctly. This spacious and open space in our heart-mind is said in Buddhism to be like a mirror. The quality of the mirror is that it reflects all things, equally. Awareness is a place inside us that is ever-healed, untouched by the past. It is the wisdom place inside us, empty of concepts, completely open. Knowing this place, we don't have to chase elephants. We are content to rest and discover the Great Perfection of life as it unfolds.

ʔ ʔ ʔ

Endnotes

1.   Roshi Bernie Tetsugan Glassman, private talk, Zen Community, New York, 1985.

7

Finding Elephants

There is a Zen koan which asks, "Show me your face before 'you' were born." This is asking us to discover our unborn, unmanifest, formless awareness, always full of potential before the separate sense of "I" and "you" occurred, before the bifurcation of subject and object began. In Buddhism there is nothing in nature that is independent or permanent. All forms in nature are interdependent and impermanent. To the degree that we experience ourselves as separate and independent and permanent, we see that we are involved in a fabrication of the mind, a construction of the mind.

When we look at the spiritual question "What is this life?" we are left speechless and not knowing. This gap of space in not knowing is pure awareness. This is the place that healing begins.

Buddhism speaks of the interdependence, of form and emptiness, relative and absolute, form and formless, manifest and unmanifest. We are ultimately that which is imperceptible to the senses, that unattached formlessness, the awareness of all and everything, in which there are no problems. Yet we are also that which objectifies into subject and object in which there are constant problems. Understanding that we manifest as this form and that the manifest and the unmanifest are interdependent helps us not to be so identified with this form and to think it is the totality of who we are.

If we decide we want to live as we truly are, then our pain will have to be gone through over and over as we declare our inner truth in a world accustomed to people pleasing others or following conventional prescriptions for living. The pain comes from the piercing of old wounds from childhood in which our truth, our very presence, was not appreciated, recognized, and loved. Telling our truth at last as it arises activates our wounds from childhood, but ultimately frees us from the bondage of somebody else's ideas of who we are. Like all great things, becoming real is simple…but definitely not easy.

An aspect of wisdom that Buddhism teaches is that the universe supports us in our healing journey. The universe is supportive to us in teaching us through the breath that we cannot hold on to anything. If you try to cling to your breath, you will die. So the breath is one of the great constant metaphors for things coming to us to bring us life without any effort at all on our part, yet we cannot hold on to it.

Our true nature wants to reveal itself. We see this in our longing to live as we are, to be free, to return home, to be true to ourselves, to know the truth of how things work in reality. The action of staying with ourself no matter what brings us our inner wisdom, which teaches us that even though we might have been abandoned as children, we are never going to abandon ourself.

One of the most important ways that we can use the Buddhist wisdom teachings is to see the importance of living our life in the present moment. The value of staying present with yourself no matter what happens, no matter how you are hurting in a situation, is something that takes trust that in the universe things happen as they are meant to happen with a design that keeps the planet going. We can speak to clients about the great wound that occurred when they were abandoned emotionally in childhood, when they were not recognized, when they were not mirrored, when their precious being was not seen, and this means that if they do these things to themselves, there will be the same kind of pain perpetuated.

Most clients live in the past or the future most of the time. As J. J. Krishnamurti used to teach, we are not present in our life.[1]

We are not present in our relationships. We live our relationships a lot in our memory of the person and what they did to us in the past or in the grip of our self-images, which are only stories. We live in our ideas of how relationships should be. We live in our images of who we think we are. Just staying present with the illumination of our attention allows us to see what is happening clearly. *We are not stuck with anything unless we cling to it. Everything is workable.*

When we are wise, we are intimate with our own experience and we are connected with our own heart. It takes great courage and clarity to understand and digest the truth of one's own subjectivity and to allow it to stretch beyond our self-concepts from childhood. Our wisdom comes in not only seeing the value of our own subjectivity but having the courage to stay present as it shifts and transforms without thinking we know how it's going to turn out.

There is a great wisdom and understanding that what you really are is what is happening right now. It's just right here. That's why it works instantly to become more present.

Ramana Maharshi, one of the world's great spiritual teachers, used to say that this fullness we are seeking is within. It is the elephant we've been chasing. Franz Kafka, in a poem, put it this way:

> You don't need to leave your room.
> Remain sitting at your table and listen.
> Don't even wait.
> Be quite still and solitary.
>   The world will freely offer
>   itself to you
> To be unmasked, it has no choice.
> It will roll in ecstasy at your feet.[2]

As we stay present and surrender into the moment, the world will freely offer itself to us, and as we truly see it, our inner wisdom opens. As the eye of wisdom opens, we will see this beauty, this wonder, this perfection of being the only way we can be and how lovely that is. We see the Buddha within everyone's presence, their "isness," their unique "suchness."

In each of us is the awakeness, dance of consciousness, love, clarity, infinite awareness, space, light, peacefulness, compassion, and wisdom of the Buddha who lived 2,500 years ago. People study Buddhism, understanding that they can also realize the freedom and wisdom and compassion within that the Buddha found. The first part of this process is to turn toward yourself and know yourself deeply from inside.

Our source within, our true human nature, brings us everything in the universe for it is all within our awareness waiting to emerge when we are willing to stay present. We are lacking nothing when we stop chasing elephants and see what's in us. We realize the elephant is inside of us — the jewel everyone looks for. We are the fullness we've been seeking. Appreciating this is our wisdom.

We all have to learn to be still enough to receive and mindfully recognize the new moment as it spontaneously arises. *The problem with discursive thinking is that we are not inwardly quiet enough to receive the new moment and to see it for the perfection it is.* We discover in Buddhist practice that love is as is, it doesn't ask for anything to be different. And love and awareness have the same quality as they move through us. We are too busy to notice the beauty of all around and in us.

By staying so focused on discursive thinking, conditioned concepts and stories, psychotherapy has often missed seeing what is most alive in the moment. The best therapy occurs in the here and now. This form of awareness practice in therapy is the same as spiritual practice, but since everything in the universe is interdependent, it makes perfect sense that this would be so. The awareness of nowness is our Buddha nature in spiritual practice and in psychotherapy and in daily life. This is precisely how we naturally connect with our health and bring ourselves into spontaneous aliveness. The openness of this state of awareness brings us whatever potential we need to be whole. We shine the light of awareness onto whatever we have and our feelings and thoughts know they've been heard. They are content and they dissolve.

When you enter the moment as it is arising and you are one with it, so are you full, so are you complete, so you are healing. What could be missing in a moment when you are fully in it? When you are fully present in a moment what is lacking?

As Sogyal Rinpoche said in the *Tibetan Book of Living and Dying*:

"So where exactly is this Buddha nature? It is in the skylike nature of our mind. Utterly open, free, and limitless, it is fundamentally so simple and so natural that it can never be complicated, corrupted, or stained, so pure that it is beyond even the concept of purity and impurity. As it is said: `It is simply your flawless present awareness, cognizant and empty, naked and awake.'"3

When Buddha realized his true nature twenty-five hundred years ago, people asked him what type of special person he was. They asked him if he was an avatar, and he said, "No, I am a human being." But they wanted to know what kind of human being he was since he seemed so extraordinary, and he said, "I am awake." He then became known as the Buddha, which means "the awakened one."

It didn't just happen to somebody 2,500 years ago. One of the things it means to be awake is to know that you can choose to be free at any moment in time by laying aside your story and choosing to come into the Now. You can wake up and create new choices any moment you wish. Experiencing our true human nature along with our conditioned personality is knowing the whole person we are. To choose to be free, to come into the Now, is being responsible for our own life. To come home over and over to our breath, to our eyes and ears, to our awareness in the now, is the practice of awakening. This is the most profound healing process I know.

Buddha knew that if we will let ourselves be, we will be happy and full. There is nothing we have to add or take away from our true human nature. It is all there waiting to be revealed. Whatever stories we cling to that cause us un-happiness are not our essential being, our true human nature which is untouched by any distress of our past. We have a pure, open, spacious home within that is always fresh and alive. It is our Being and our awareness. We have to learn to go there for refuge. It is where the elephant rests at our hearth.

Since we have Buddha nature, we can learn to live with awareness and change our perception of the possible. We can come right into the now by focusing on our breath, and then bring our awareness to what's happening in the frame right in front of us now. This is Buddha's key to freedom from suffering. "The truth will set you free" is the wisdom teaching of seeing things as they are, and staying present and open moment to moment.

An honest getting down to what is happening here and now will reveal that "being intimate is closer to you than your very self," as Nisargadatta Maharaj, the great Indian Advaita Vedanta teacher, said.[4] Staying open, letting it be, and recognizing how it is, is the way home. It brings us to our natural flow, our contentment, and ease. It offers us our inher-ent wisdom. In being present as is, in contact with our unborn, undying nature, with awareness that holds it all, we and the elephant are one!

Endnotes

1. J. J. Krishnamurti, *The Wholeness of Life* (San Francisco: Harper and Row, 1979), p. 91.

2. Franz Kafka, from a poem posted from a seminar with Lama Surya Das, Canandaigua, New York, 1998. Unknown source.

3. Sogyal Rinpoche, *Tibetan Book of Living and Dying* (San Francisco: Harper and Row, 1994), p. 49.

4. Nisargadatta Maharaj, *I Am That* (Durham, NC: Acorn Press, 1986), p. 467.

8

Healing Into the Invisible Body of Truth

S eeing that there is nothing to grasp leaves us open to the *process* of living. More than that, it leaves us appreciating that nothing lasts, and right here is it. As we heal, we make contact with the larger totality that we are, until as J. J. Krishnamurti taught, we are the World — we are one with *all* there is, intimate with whatever is in front of us.

I spent many weekends practicing Zen in delis and grocery stores on the Upper West Side of Manhattan wearing my baker's apron and setting up a stand for baked products and bread from Greyston Bakery. My Zen practice was partly to introduce people who passed to Greyston Bakery products, which was the Zen Community of New York's livelihood at the time. People asked me if I was a baker, and I told them I was a Zen student working for the monastery. I got a similar positive response when I was a graduate student working as a waitress in the Catskills weekends and holidays. People would ask me if I was going to school and what I was studying. I told them I was studying to be a psychologist. Some told me they got a kick out of being served by a "Jewish doctor."

On Saturday after early morning zazen practice a crew of us would go out on the street in Yonkers in the filthy factory neighborhood and clean the streets. We swept and cleaned up trash. I was often cold, and preferred the indoor job of mopping the bakery floor. So, of course, I was sent outside to clean the street. An all-night bar in Yonkers next door to the zendo contributed its late-night trash including liquor bottles, dope needles, and endless crushed cigarettes. When I got involved in it I forgot who was sweeping. I would ask, "Who is it that wants to have a nice clean work practice?" There was no immediate answer.

I called Roshi Glassman once and asked him if I could come to the zendo for a couple of weeks. There was some feeling of immanence, some push to seeing through something. I came up from Manhattan that afternoon. The zendo was in the bakery, a training center for homeless men and women. I slept on the floor in a small office in my sleeping bag, and was content. Roshi Glassman said to me one day as I was sweeping the steps in the bakery, "You'll never forget this time for the rest of your life." He was right.

Whenever they put me in a spiritual context I was crying or laughing: in the United Hebrew Temple, listening to music, in Sandra Eisenstein's loft when we said prayers from the Rig Veda, at Krishnamurti's grove in Ojai in stillness, at Rabbi Don Singer's Shabbat service, at Father Kennedy's offering the blood of Christ at Catholic mass. I laughed and cried at the Zikr with Lex Hixon. I cried at the magnificent Taisho's of Roshi Berni Glassman through the years. I cry with patients as they come into their heart.

For the past five years in the summer I sit with Lama Surya Das. I sit in a chair outside and look at the sky, look out into open space, the summer sun radiating everywhere. I sit for hours absorbed in pure presence. Moving into nondual awareness opens the heart. I sit with Tsokyni Rinpoche summers at Wisdom House in Connecticut. The students sit in the meditation hall for early morning service and many go to sit outside. I sit on a chair on a porch overlooking a grove of trees with vast stretches of space and sky all around. Some fifty feet away are several buildings where people stay for the retreat. I stay on the porch and watch people coming and going, the leaves moving, wind softly blowing, the light shifting. I am in bliss for hours in the morning on the porch. Who is meditating? Everything spontaneously arises in the great perfection where people come and go, thoughts come and go. Everything comes and goes spontaneously: light, trees, wind, sound. The six senses left in their natural state is resting the weary mind…is natural great peace.

I have an appointment with my meditation cushion and with the birds outside my window most early mornings. They sing their heart out to me in all seasons. I watch them happily fly freely in the trees. I have remembered this place of early morning awareness practice all over the world. It is my place of refuge inside. Here I am free and at peace, content and present. This pure, loving presence has never been touched by my grief and fear. It is where I come from and return to. I see this place of awareness as who I am. I want to express the gratitude I have for this Buddha nature within. The gratitude led me to open my home for meditation practice weekly. It led me to become a Zen priest. In my house I have a lovely room with a big window. It is a space for entering the silence and meditating. I invite people to join me or they come on their own. I want to share the great silence with others. People ask me what I do as a Buddhist priest. "I practice coming home," I say. I know where to find the space within where elephants and all other creatures abide.

I didn't want to go to Auschwitz with the Zen Peacemaker order and Roshi Glassman to do a retreat. I didn't know much about the Holocaust, beyond what I had read or seen in movies. I was afraid of the cold of Poland, the images of horror. What decided me to go was unknown. I still don't know. There was an impulse to be a part of it but it wasn't conceptual. I began to read books on the reading list for the Auschwitz retreat and found myself open and responsive. It was immediately apparent when the 150 people came together from all over the United States and Europe to meet that each person was on a private inner journey. Mine wasn't yet apparent to me.

There were people from every walk of life who had family in the Holocaust, whose families were Nazis, who had lost family, who were from territories around the camps, who had some personal involvement. Why was I here? As I trudged out to the grim November grounds of Birkenau I was deep inside without concepts. I felt a part of some force without any particular ideas. The place Auschwitz had taken away my ideas. I felt like nobody in particular. I went to the Holocaust Museum to see the personal effects of the dead. I began to feel the strong yearning for family that I had lost over the years. I had left my family at twenty-one seldom to return. My children had left home in growing up. I felt deeply lonely and longing for a family to belong to. Listening to the names of the dead we recited each day, listening to one person after another speak at night, I began to feel a sense of connection with everyone.

I shared a tarp with Enkyo O'Hara, a Buddhist teacher from New York City. We put our meditation pillows on top of it. Bob Sherwood from Denmark had come for the retreat and we carried foam rubber out to put our tarps on to protect them from snow and rain. I couldn't come up with any conclusions about all of this violence and love all around me. How can we violate so when we love so? We came together as the family I had lost. Then one night I saw with blazing clarity the concentration camp I had built inside my mind. Now twenty years later I still was imprisoned by ideas of how a family was supposed to be, and how mine wasn't. I was behind the barbed wire of my judgments, my rigid, insane ideas about mothering, about family. My whole life I had been trying to prove something — to avoid freedom, to deny love, to live with ideas of right and wrong. I saw how I always felt I wasn't enough.

On the night I got up to speak I was choked up. I spoke of how I had done violence my whole life inside the concentration camp I had built in my mind. "Not good enough" was the verdict, and I had exterminated my loving heart. I had exterminated my freedom to be me my whole life. Each time anyone spoke there was stone silence before, then after…simply this looking…facing the way we hurt each other and ourselves so violently every day. What brutality we commit. How much we love behind all that hurt. Suddenly I was the woman lining up to go to the gas chambers, holding my children's hands. I overflowed with feelings of how that was, those stoking the fires and those walking into them. I walked in and felt the heat of my own hatred for myself, then the love underneath it began arising.

Sitting in the falling snow the next day as we said our prayers, waves of light poured from the sky. The sky was everywhere. I saw that love is everywhere, is our Buddha nature. I sat flooded with the light of the sky, worlds within worlds, and my heart broken open. From the depths of human violence had come forth joy and ecstasy in me that afternoon and a realization of the true family we are in as human creatures. Bearing witness was opening into healing within me. I saw that no matter what happens there is this light, this breath, this life force, this love that unites us all. Without any ideas, we can love each other just for being who we are. Roshi Glassman had invited me to Auschwitz. I had accepted the invitation and had found the family I had been searching for my whole life.

The vast November sky around the death camp was wide open, showered with falling snow and light. Even the concentration camp rested in the grace of afternoon snow. There at Auschwitz, in the concentration camp, I found the deepest gratitude possible for our intimate connection with each other, for our willingness to bear witness to one another, and for the natural way we heal when we face exactly where we are.

We heal from that source from which everything arises. We heal into the radiant mystery into which it returns. All we have to do to get into this flow of healing is to give up our self-concepts. Everything passes when we choose not to cling to them. In each moment we can choose to let things be and see that life renews itself, re-creates itself naturally, in a flow of healing that is indeed wise.

Tony lost his wife weeks ago. He sat with me, and said, "I'm tearing at this. The whys. What I did, wanting to do it right. I think I did it wrong. My mind won't leave me alone."

He is quiet, and says, "I keep wanting to make a poem out of this to give my kids…but there are no words. I miss Anne with every atom. But I can't cry. I won't let my heart break. I can't."

"What are you experiencing now, Tony?"

"Nothing. I want to be left alone. I want to be quiet."

"Okay."

"I have nothing. I'm afraid you'll leave."

"You can only be yourself."

"Please," he says, his voice stops.

I say quietly, "Just this much… Touch yourself with the truth in you."

We sit in silence about twenty minutes. Tony looks out the window at the large tree branches barren in the winter cold. He stares at the sky. I join him in this process of reflecting in silence. Then Tony says, "I feel a presence with us."

"Yes," I say.

Tony says, "I wasn't thinking." Tears fill his eyes, and then he says, "I keep saying the Jesus prayer."

"That's beautiful," I say.

Tony says, "Can we say it?"

"Yes." We repeat the prayer several times. "Lord Jesus Christ, Son of God, have mercy on me, a sinner." Then there is silence. We sit a few moments together, and Tony says "I feel better." He walks over to get his hat and coat on the couch. He looks into my eyes, he says thanks, and leaves.

Stillness and our being together moves us into pure being, pure presence. For many reasons, he trusts us being together enough to go inside and be still. We are both healing in the Invisible body of Truth: Pure Presence.

ஜ   ஜ   ஜ

After all words have failed, we open into a space that embodies pure mystery and surrenders into "Thy will be done." This is the space of awareness where we come home to being without having to figure it out, where we are supported by our awareness as it moves naturally.

Gangaji, a dharma heir of Ramana Maharshi, said,

> If you tell the truth and are very attentive to silence a profound discovery is revealed. You are home.[1]

Tony is aware of how he is trapped in his mind and can't stop judging himself for his wife's dying. Giving himself a space to be, returning to pure presence, his anguish is self-liberated into prayer. He is falling away from some of his concepts about life. Rumi describes this process in many of his poems. For example:

> The way of love is not a subtle argument
> The door there is devastation
>
> Birds make great sky-circles of
>   their freedom.
> How do they learn it?
> They fall and falling they're
>   given wings.[2]

At some point, Tony mentioned that a sense of presence had come into the room. Everything was happening the way it was supposed to, even though grief was there too. Awareness held the grief in an open embrace and opened us naturally into love and joy. The skylike awareness at Auschwitz, had held all of our grief on the retreat and transformed it into Truth.

Tony and I were in the presence of the sacred as it came without any effort. "It" fell upon us, bringing us both a sense of fullness and peace. We both accepted the invitation of presence to just be. The door there indeed was devastation. It had led us to "the way of love."

We meet the Buddha within our awareness of nowness. We find our inner treasure by staying present no matter where we started and we end up meeting the bliss of our own Being. Staying present in the flow of our experience reveals the truth of where we are inside and is the most powerful healing. In this manner we find our way back home inside. To be present with the rhythm of someone spontaneously, naturally unfolding, is the heart of healing. From this place of pure presence we sit contentedly next to the elephant. We can be with ourself and with all the other creatures in the universe enjoying the show.

"Make use of this spaciousness, this freedom
and natural ease.
Don't search any further.
Don't go into the tangled jungle
Looking for the great awakened elephant
Who is already resting quietly at home
In front of your own hearth.
Nothing to do or undo, nothing to force,
Nothing to want and nothing missing...
Emaho! Marvelous!
Everything happens by itself."[3]

So we are not chasing elephants anymore. Our journey deepens and we make friends with the elephant within ourself, the wisdom within. The journey within deepens and opens until there's nothing missing. *Emaho*! Marvelous! Enjoy the elephant who is resting quietly at home in front of your own hearth. Look, see, let be, and be free. We rest in comfort and in ease. We see our inner jewel and carefully wrap it up in our heart cloth. We cherish it. Then we share it with everyone.

Any place on a path toward discovering who we truly are is a blessing. Psychotherapy can play an important part in this discovery. So can spiritual work. So can everyday life.

I'm so grateful that for some unknown reason my part in the dance is to light up this path a few moments for a few who have chosen to travel the Way.

Endnotes

1.   Satsang with Gangaji, *You Are That!*, Vol. 1, (Gangaji, 1995), p. 66.

2.   Rumi, *Birdsong*, trans. Coleman Barks (Athens, GA: Maypop, 1993), p. 13.

3.   Nyoshul Khenpo Rinpoche and Lama Surya Das, *op. cit.*, *Natural Great Perfection*, pp. 11-12.

Bibliography

Almaas, A. H. *The Pearl Beyond Price*. Berkeley, CA: Diamond Books, 1988.

_____. *Diamond Heart — Book I*. Berkeley, CA: Diamond Heart Books, 1993.

Balsekar, Ramesh, S. *Sri Nisargadatta Maharaj: Pointers from Nisargadatta Maharaj*. Durham, NC: Acorn Press 1982.

Beck, Charlotte Joko. *Everyday Zen*. San Francisco: Harper, 1989.

Chödrön, Pema. *Start Where You Are*. Boston: Shambhala Publications, 1994.

Chopra, Deepak. *The Seven Spiritual Laws of Success*. San Rafael, CA: Amber-Allen Publishing, 1994.

Das, Lama Surya. *Awakening the Buddha Within*. New York: Broadway Books, 1997.

_____. Guided meditation. Dzogchen retreat, Canandaigua, New York, summer 1995, 1996, and 1997.

_____. Guided meditation. Winter retreat, Dover, MA, 1998.

Dayanda, Swami. Talk on Vedanta. Arsha Ashram, Saylorsville, PA. October 1989.

Dhammapada, The Sayings of Buddha. Rendered by Thomas Byrom. Boston & London: Shambhala, 1993.

Eliot, T. S. *Four Quartets, Part III*. *The Collected Poems of T. S. Eliot*.

Feng, Gia-Fu, and English, Jane, trans. *Tao Te Ching*. New York: Vintage Books, 1989.

Foundation for Inner Peace. *A Course in Miracles*. 1985.

Gendlin, Eugene. *Focusing*. New York: Bantam Books, 1982.

Glassman, Roshi Bernard Tetsugan, and Mathiesson, Peter Muryo, Trans. *Heart Sutra*. New York: Sutra Books, Zen Center of New York, 1985.

_____. Private talk. Zen Community Center, New York, 1985.

Greenberg, Jay R. and Mitchell, Stephen A. *Object Relations in Psychoanalytic Theory*. Cambridge, MA and London, England: Harvard University Press, 1983.

Hixon, Lex. *Living Buddha Zen*. Burdett, NY: Larson Publications, 1995.

John, Da Free. *The Holy Jumping Off Place*. San Rafael, CA: The Dawn Horse Press, 1986.

_____. Home study course.

Johnson, Alia. A statement from a Diamond Heart class. New York City, 1996.

Kafka, Franz. From a poem posted from a seminar with Lama Surya Das. Canandaigua, NY, 1998.

Khenpo, Nyoshul. *Natural Great Perfection*. Trans. by Lama Surya Das. Ithaca, NY: Snow Lion Publications, 1995.

Krishnamurti, J. J. *The Wholeness of Life*. San Francisco, CA: Harper & Row, 1979.

Levine, Stephen. Talks given on healing at Omega Institute. Rhinebeck, NY. Summer 1992.

Longchempa, "Cloud Banks of Nector," *Crystal Cave*. Trans. from Tibetan by Erik Pema Junsang. Kathmandu, Hong Kong: Rangjung Yeshe, 1990.

Maharaj, Nisargadatta. *I Am That*. Durham, NC: Acorn Press, 1992.

Ngondro, Dudjom Tersar. *Ngondro Practice*. New York: Yeshe Melong, 1992.

Noh, Jae Jah. *Do You See What I See? A Message from a Mystic*. Quest Books.

Notes from a summer retreat with Lama Surya Das. Canandaigua, NY, 1997.

Norbu, Namkhai. *Dzogchen: The Self-Perfected State*. Ithaca, NY: Snow Lion Publications, 1996.

Poonja, H. W. L. *Wake Up and Roar*. Vol. 2. Kula Maui, HI: Pacific Center Press, 1993.

Powell, Robert. Editor. *Sri Nisargadatta Maharaj: The Nectar of Immortality*. San Diego, CA: Blue Dove Press, 1996.

Rangdrol, Tsele Natsok. *The Heart of the Matter*. Hong Kong: Rangjung Yeshe Publications, 19__.

Rinpoche, Nyoshul Khenpo and Das, Lama Surya. *Natural Great Perfection*. Ithaca, NY: Snow Lion Publications, 1995.

Rinpoche, Sogyal. *The Tibetan Book of Living and Dying*. New York: Harper Collins, 1994.

Rogers, Carl. *I Am, Then I Change*. Boston, MA: Houghton Mifflin Co., 1961.

Roshi, Maezumi. Public talk. New York City, 1980.

Rumi. *Birdsong. 53 Short Poems*. Trans. by Coleman Barks. Athens, GA: Maypop, 1993.

Satsang with Gangaji. *You Are That! Vol. 1*. Gangaji, 1995.

Shainberg, Diane. *Healing in Psychotherapy: The Process of Holistic Change*. New York: Gordon and Breach, 1983.

_____. Poem from guided imagery class. New York City, 1995.

_____. Class on integrating spirit into psychotherapy practice.

Shorter Oxford English Dictionary, 3rd ed. London: Oxford University Press, Amen House, 1956.

Suzuki, Shunryo. *Zen Mind, Beginner's Mind.* New York:
Weatherhill, Inc., 1997.

ABOUT THE AUTHOR

DIANE SHAINBERG, Ph.D., is a psychotherapist in New York City and Director of The Mani Center for Integral Psychotherapy and Study. She has been a student of Zen and Dzogchen Buddhism for more than thirty years.

She has studied Advaita Vedanta with Ramesh Balsekar and teaches psychotherapists, counselors, healers, and others how to integrate the non-dual awareness teachings and practices of Zen and Dzogchen Buddhism and Advaita Vedanta into their life and work.

As an ordained Zen Buddhist Priest, Dr. Shainberg leads a meditation group at the Carnegie Hill Zen Center in Manhattan, New York. She is a member of the Peacemaker Community, founded and directed by Roshi Bernie Glassman, and she conducts a monthly Dzogchen group for Lama Surya Das.

She has written numerous articles and two books: *Healing in Psychotherapy: The Process of Holistic Change* and *The Path and Process of Inner Change*, and has won several awards for her writing. She has a Ph.D in clinical psychology from Columbia University.

Dr. Shainberg offers an on-going training program in Integral Psychotherapy at the Mani Center in New York City, along with workshops on the Integration of Meditation, and psychological and spiritual transformative work. For information, please contact:

Diane Shainberg
The Mani Center for Integral Psychotherapy
124 East 95th Street
New York, New York 10128
Phone: (212) 876-8213
Fax: (212) 722-8062

Additional copies of *CHASING ELEPHANTS* are
available from:

ASTI-RAHMAN BOOKS
P.O. Box 674
New York, NY 10028-0044

$16.95 for softbound edition, plus $3.50 shipping and
handling for the first copy ($1.50 each additional copy)
and sales tax for NY orders.